EATING WELL
IN A BUSY WORLD

Well balanced, healthful meals
for busy people who love to cook.

EATING WELL IN A BUSY WORLD

FRANCINE ALLEN

With illustrations by
RUTH ANNE MARTIN

Ten Speed Press

TEN SPEED PRESS
P.O. Box 7123
Berkeley, California 94707

Library of Congress Catalog Number: 85–052164
ISBN: 0–89815–163–5

Book design by Nancy Austin
Cover design by Brenton Beck
Illustrations by Ruth Anne Martin
Composition by Wilsted & Taylor

Printed in the United States of America
10   9   8   7   6   5   4   3   2   1

Table of Contents

**TIME TO
PREPARE**

CHICKEN DISHES

FISH DISHES

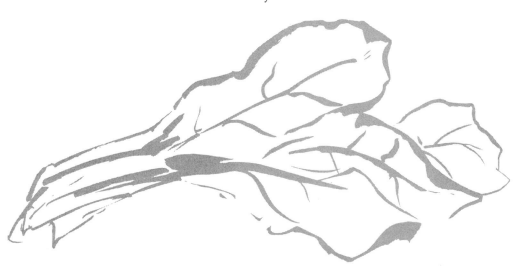

PAGE	TIME TO PREPARE	

MEET DISHES

Introduction

This cookbook was conceived where probably the majority of modern ideas are born—in the automobile. Each day on my way home from work I knew that soon I would be confronted with the problem of preparing dinner. The evening meal, I realized while driving along the sinuous and darkly wooded road that leads to my home, is when I want to delight in the sensual bounty of the earth, gather myself, and nurture and be nurtured by my family and friends seated around the table. But I am always so tired by the time I get home!

I first sought a solution in the "quick-and-easy" cookbook sections of several bookstores, but I could not find what I wanted. This apparent void, and my having worked as a cook in different capacities and as a staff writer for a magazine that focused on health, technology and environment, precipitated the decision to write a cookbook. It seemed a useful service, and I was curious to see just how hard and successfully I could work at developing an *excellent* "quick-and-easy" cookbook.

One of the most useful things I feel a cookbook can do for the tired cook is to preplan and "think through" meal preparation; making decisions with a brain worn smooth as a stone that's been in a tumbler all day is miserable. Developing the format of this book became very important. Rather than listing single recipes, it is organized into complete meals. Each menu is laid out so that it is visually easy to follow; cooks can see at a glance how long a meal will take to prepare, what ingredients they need to shop for, and how to most efficiently use their preparation time.

One of the simplest ways I have found to refresh myself from the numbness caused by long hours of shuffling ideas and papers is to immerse myself in the textures, colors and smells of things of the earth. By the time I get home, it may be so dark outside that I cannot see the trees; but, when I slice open an acorn squash it wakes me, and makes me feel good in a way that going to a restaurant or popping a frozen meal into the oven cannot. In developing these menus, I have assumed that rinsing, chopping and cooking fresh foods not only leads to healthful meals, but can sensually delight and mentally relax the tired cook.

Preparation times are based on how long the meal takes me to prepare it without the aid of a food processor. Until you get the hang of some of these recipes, you may find that some of the meals take a few minutes longer than the indicated time to prepare.

The recipes minimize the use of fats, oils, red meat, butter, cheese, eggs and sugar, and maximize the use of whole grains and fresh vegetables. A third of the menus feature chicken, a third feature fish and a third are vegetarian. (There are three exceptions: two recipes include sausage and one recipe is for stir-fried beef. These dishes were too good to leave out.) In the index you will find individual recipes for particular ingredients you may have on hand.

There are no recipes for dessert; I would suggest serving fresh fruit. There is a section on "Techniques of Quick Cooking" and collections of recipes for salad dressings, for sauces, and for breakfasts. Some of the breakfast recipes are based on traditional desserts—cobblers and puddings, for instance. I believe that it is a treat and is healthier to prepare these dishes with less butter and sweetener and to enjoy them as a tasty morning meal, than to eat them in a rich and sweetened form following a full evening meal.

Finally, nearly all the cooking is done on the top of the stove, which saves energy. Because the recipes do not generally use cream or lots of cheese or butter, or prepackaged mixes or expensive cuts of meat, you will find these meals are economical to prepare. Research into the cooking styles of different cultures provided unusually seasoned recipes; the kitchen is one place where international politics doesn't interfere with our celebrating the world's cultures.

That is the why and how of this book. May it serve you well.

INVERNESS, CALIFORNIA

Acknowledgments

I originally published a version of this manuscript myself under the title *International Menus for the Busy, Health-Conscious Cook*. The acknowledgments read:

"A hearty thank you to the many friends in the Tomales Bay community for their assistance, support and participation in this project. You'd be surprised how much even a smiling nod of encouragement helped. A special thanks to: Janet Allen, who gave me a great boost towards making the publication of this book possible; Jane Borchers, who advised me in the technical aspects of nutrition, proofread the first draft, and encouraged me to continue; Dave Brast, who could teach my software to jump through hoops, but alas, not me; Mary Eubank, who served as test kitchen and taster, gave me some excellent recipes, and months of patient listening; Fred Graeser, who inspired me with a copy of his own homecooked book, and amidst the ebullience of his laughter and generosity, helped me lay out mine; Ruth Anne Martin, who could magically give me back laughter and determination when I'd run out, and Richard, technician, ballast and mate."

There are a few more people who have played special roles in the making of this book I wish to thank: George Young, editor at Ten Speed, for his cheerful kindness; Jackie Wan, Ten Speed's copyeditor, for maintaining her indefatigable attention to detail and just plain working so hard; and to Cathe Howe, who wrote a review of the self-published version of the manuscript for the *Pacific Sun*, which became the catalyst for transforming it into its present form.

EATING WELL
IN A BUSY WORLD

CHICKEN DISHES

Chicken Chasseur (Hunter's Chicken)

Parmesan Noodles

Tossed Greens with Vinaigrette Dressing

SERVES 4

TIME TO PREPARE

60 minutes

INGREDIENTS

ON HAND

- ☐ *butter*
- ☐ *olive oil*
- ☐ *wine vinegar*
- ☐ *dry white wine*
- ☐ *fresh garlic*
- ☐ *thyme*

SHOPPING LIST

- ☐ *1 small chicken*
- ☐ *1 yellow onion*
- ☐ *3 green onions*
- ☐ *¼ lb. fresh mushrooms*
- ☐ *fresh parsley*
- ☐ *salad greens for 4*
- ☐ *12 oz. egg noodles*
- ☐ *1 16-oz. can whole peeled tomatoes*
- ☐ *2 oz. Parmesan cheese (½ cup)*

OVERVIEW

1. Begin to broil the chicken. Prepare the sauce. Simmer chicken in sauce.

2. Bring water to a boil to cook noodles. Prepare the salad and dressing. (*See page 100 for Vinaigrette Dressings.*) Cover and chill the salad greens until ready to toss with dressing and serve.

3. Time the noodles to finish cooking when the chicken is ready to serve. Serve the chicken and chasseur sauce over the noodles. Garnish with parsley and Parmesan cheese.

Chicken Chasseur

1 small chicken, rinsed and cut into pieces

1 tablespoon olive oil

2 tablespoons dry white wine

3 green onions, sliced, stems included

4 tablespoons chopped yellow onion

2 large cloves garlic, minced

¼ lb. fresh mushrooms, sliced

½ tablespoon leaf thyme

½ cup dry white wine

1 16-oz. can whole peeled tomatoes, drained

1 tablespoon chopped fresh parsley

freshly grated Parmesan cheese

Place the chicken skin–side up in a broiler pan. Broil for 7 minutes. Turn and broil for another 5 minutes. As the chicken broils prepare the sauce. Heat the olive oil and wine; sauté the onions and garlic until soft. Meanwhile, wash and slice the mushrooms. Add the mushrooms and thyme to the skillet. Cover and cook 5 minutes. Stir in ½ cup wine and the tomatoes, breaking up the tomatoes into small pieces. Bring to a simmer. Place the chicken in the skillet and spoon the sauce over it. Cover and simmer 15 minutes. Remove the lid and simmer 10 minutes to reduce liquid. Season with salt and freshly ground pepper to taste. Garnish with Parmesan and parsley.

Parmesan Noodles

12 oz. egg noodles

1 tablespoon butter

4 tablespoons freshly grated Parmesan cheese

Bring to boil a large pot of water; boil the noodles until *al dente*. Drain in colander. Put 1 tablespoon butter in the cooking pot. Rinse noodles under hot running water. Drain well and return to pot. Toss. Add Parmesan cheese. Toss. Season with salt and freshly ground pepper.

Tossed Green Salad with Vinaigrette Dressing

See page 100 for instructions.

Green Chili Chicken Enchiladas
Crisp Green Bean Salad

SERVES 4

TIME TO PREPARE

45 minutes

INGREDIENTS

ON HAND
☐ *flour*
☐ *vegetable oil*
☐ *red wine vinegar*
☐ *fresh garlic*
☐ *basil*
☐ *1 hard-boiled egg (optional)*
☐ *chicken stock (1 cup, optional)*

SHOPPING LIST
☐ *5 chicken breast halves*
☐ *½ lb. fresh green beans*
☐ *1 carrot*
☐ *celery*
☐ *1 yellow onion*
☐ *1 small red onion*
☐ *fresh parsley*
☐ *1 dozen corn tortillas*
☐ *1 4-oz. can diced green chilies*
☐ *1 28-oz. can whole peeled tomatoes*
☐ *10 oz. Farmer's or Jack cheese*
☐ *Optional garnishes for enchiladas:*
  avocado
  1 lime
  green onions
  cilantro
  black olives
  sour cream

This recipe makes enough green chili sauce for approximately 12 enchiladas. Freeze leftover sauce in one or more plastic containers; the next time you want to have enchiladas, just pop the frozen sauce out of the container and bring to a simmer. With the sauce already made, this meal takes only 30 minutes to prepare. A half chicken breast will stuff 2 to 3 enchiladas. The enchiladas are equally good stuffed with refried beans and cheese or sautéed ground turkey rather than chicken. In making the sauce, replace the poaching liquid with either chicken stock or vegetable broth. Proceed as above, but lay a generous spoonful of refried beans or sautéed ground turkey, cheese and sauce across each tortilla.

♦ Refried Beans and Cheese—2 cups homemade refried beans or a 15-oz. can will stuff approximately 10 enchiladas.

♦ Turkey—1 ¼ lb. ground turkey will stuff 12 enchiladas. Sauté the meat with 2 to 4 tablespoons of sauce; season with ½ teaspooon cumin and ¼ teaspoon coriander if desired.

OVERVIEW

1. Prepare the Green Bean Salad as the chicken breasts are poaching.

2. Prepare the enchilada sauce. Preheat the oven to 350°. As the sauce simmers, prepare remaining ingredients for enchiladas. Assemble and bake 15 minutes. Garnish and serve.

Crisp Green Bean Salad

½ lb. green beans

1 carrot, coarsely grated

1 stalk of celery, chopped

1 hard-boiled egg, chopped (optional)

MARINADE

1 small red onion, thinly sliced

1 clove garlic, pressed

¼ cup red wine vinegar

⅓ cup vegetable oil

½ teaspoon salt

freshly ground pepper to taste

2 tablespoons chopped parsley

Bring about 3 cups of water to a boil. Remove ends from beans and cut into bite-sized pieces. Mix the marinade in a bowl that can hold the vegetables.

Toss green beans into boiling water. As soon as they are tender-crisp (in just a minute or two) strain them in a colander and then immediately plunge them into ice water. Pour back through the colander; shake off water, then stir the beans into the marinade along with the celery and carrot. Stir every once in a while until you are ready to serve. Garnish with chopped egg if desired.

Green Chili Chicken Enchiladas

5 chicken breast halves

1 cup chicken stock or water

SAUCE

2 tablespoons vegetable oil

1 yellow onion, chopped

2 cloves garlic, crushed

2 tablespoons flour

1 4-oz. can diced green chilies

1 28-oz. can whole peeled tomatoes, drained and chopped

1 dozen corn tortillas

10 oz. grated cheese (Farmer's or Jack)

Poach the chicken breasts gently in chicken stock or water. They will take only 10 minutes or so to cook; flip them over halfway through cooking. Remove breasts from poaching liquid; skin and bone. Shred or chop meat; set aside. Sauté the onion in oil. When soft, stir in garlic and flour. Brown for 1 minute. Stir in ½ cup poaching liquid and cook until the mixture thickens, stirring occasionally. Stir in the chilies and chopped tomatoes and simmer sauce 10 minutes.

Preheat oven to 350°. Immerse a tortilla in the sauce. Transfer to baking dish. Place a generous spoonful of grated cheese, chicken and sauce along its diameter. Fold each side towards the middle and roll it over so that it holds together. Repeat this procedure, setting one enchilada next to the other. Spoon remaining sauce and cheese over enchiladas and bake 15 minutes. Remove from oven, garnish and serve.

POSSIBLE GARNISHES

♦ chopped green onions sprinkled over slices of avocado (baked an additional 2 minutes)
♦ an avocado mashed with 1 tablespoon lime juice, ½ teaspoon chili powder, and salt to taste
♦ chopped fresh cilantro, sliced black olives, and a dab of sour cream

Moroccan Chicken Wings and Garbanzo Beans

Cucumber Salad

SERVES 4 TO 5

TIME TO PREPARE

45 minutes

INGREDIENTS

ON HAND

- ☐ *chicken stock (2 cups)*
- ☐ *cracked wheat (bulgur) or leftover cooked grain (rice, wheat or millet)*
- ☐ *butter*
- ☐ *vegetable oil*
- ☐ *fresh garlic*
- ☐ *ground coriander*
- ☐ *ground cumin*
- ☐ *ground ginger*
- ☐ *fresh or dried dill weed*

SHOPPING LIST

- ☐ *2 lbs. chicken wings*
- ☐ *2 yellow onions*
- ☐ *4 small zucchini*
- ☐ *2 medium-sized firm cucumbers*
- ☐ *fresh mint (optional)*
- ☐ *2 15-oz. cans garbanzo beans or 3 cups homecooked garbanzo beans*
- ☐ *4 to 8 oz. plain low-fat yogurt*

This recipe can easily be halved. Leftovers are delicious, however, when reheated.

OVERVIEW

Prepare the Moroccan Chicken Wings and Garbanzo Beans. During its last 5 minutes of simmering, prepare the cucumber salad.

Moroccan Chicken Wings and Garbanzo Beans

2 lbs. chicken wings

ground ginger

1 tablespoon butter

1 tablespoon vegetable oil

1 ½ cup finely chopped onion

2 cloves garlic, pressed

½ teaspoon ground cumin

2 teaspoons ground coriander

¼ teaspoon ground black pepper

½ cup raw bulgur or 1 cup cooked grains (rice, millet or wheat)

2 cups chicken stock

2 15-oz. cans garbanzo beans, drained and rinsed (or 3 cups homecooked garbanzo beans)

4 small zucchini, cut on the diagonal into ½-inch pieces

Cut off the tips of the chicken wings; wash and pat dry. (Freeze the tips to add to the stock pot.) Rub the wings with salt and ginger. Heat the oil and butter in a large heavy skillet. Brown the wings on both sides; remove from skillet. Sauté the onion until soft; stir in the garlic, spices and raw bulgur, if you are using it. Sauté for 1 minute. Add stock and wings. Bring to a boil; reduce heat and cover. Simmer 10 minutes.

Add the garbanzo beans; increase heat and bring to a simmer. Reduce heat, cover and simmer 10 minutes. (If you are using cooked, leftover grains rather than raw bulgur, stir them in now.) Place the zucchini on top. Cover and simmer for 5 minutes. Uncover and simmer another 5 minutes. Adjust seasonings to taste. Test the zucchini. If they are not yet tender, cover the skillet and continue cooking a few moments.

Cucumber Salad

2 medium-sized firm cucumbers

4 to 8 oz. plain low-fat yogurt

1 teaspoon dried dill weed or 2 teaspoons minced fresh dill weed

1 teaspoon or more minced fresh mint (if available)

salt and pepper to taste

Peel the cucumbers. Slice them in half lengthwise and scrape out the seeds. Coarsely grate the cucumbers into a bowl. Stir in the yogurt and seasonings. Serve in small individual bowls.

Szechuan-Style Chicken with Cauliflower and Broccoli

Rice or Noodles

SERVES 4

TIME TO PREPARE

30 minutes

INGREDIENTS

ON HAND
- [ ] *chicken broth (2 cups)*
- [ ] *brown rice or noodles*
- [ ] *peanut or vegetable oil*
- [ ] *fresh ginger*
- [ ] *fresh garlic*
- [ ] *cornstarch*
- [ ] *sesame seeds*

SHOPPING LIST
- [ ] *3 chicken breast halves*
- [ ] *1 bunch each cauliflower and broccoli*
- [ ] *1 red or green bell pepper*
- [ ] *2 carrots*
- [ ] *4 green onions*
- [ ] *Chinese black bean paste*
- [ ] *dried red pepper flakes*

If you are not familiar with the food from the Szechuan province of China, you may be surprised by its spiciness. Szechuan cooking is characterized by a fermented black bean paste and is permeated with garlic and hot peppers. Chinese black bean paste is available in Asian markets and gourmet shops. You may even find it, and the red pepper flakes, at your local supermarket. Do not substitute miso. An opened can of bean paste will store in the refrigerator for a very long time.

Herbalists point out that eating hot chili peppers raises the body's internal temperature and increases circulation of the blood. The result is a warming of the extremities (hands and feet), improved digestion, and the killing off of pathogens. Garlic, too, aids circulation, warms the body, and is an antiseptic. Garlic and chili peppers are used extensively in the cuisine of Third World countries and are considered as time-proven preventive medicines by millions and millions of people.

OVERVIEW

1. If you precooked rice in the morning (*see page 99 for directions*) complete cooking the rice now. If you are starting rice from scratch, allow 45 minutes for it to cook. If you don't want to wait for rice to cook, substitute noodles. Use soy, buckwheat, whole wheat or regular spaghetti noodles broken into 3-inch lengths. When *al dente*, drain, rinse and toss with a bit of oil so that they don't get sticky.

2. Thirty minutes before the rice finishes cooking, cut up the chicken and the vegetables. Stir-frying will take less than 10 minutes.

Szechuan-Style Chicken and Vegetables

3 *chicken breast halves*

8 *cups cauliflower and broccoli, cut into bite-sized pieces*

2 *carrots, sliced thin on the diagonal*

1 *green or red bell pepper cut into 1-inch squares*

3 *large green onions cut into 2-inch lengths (stems, too)*

2 *tablespoons peanut or vegetable oil*

2 *cloves garlic, peeled and thinly sliced*

¾ *teaspoon dried red pepper flakes*

1 *teaspoon grated ginger root (or more to taste)*

2 *teaspoons Chinese black bean paste*

1 ¾ *cup chicken broth*

2 *tablespoons cornstarch mixed with ¼ cup chicken broth*

GARNISH

1 *green onion, cut several times lengthwise, then crosswise into 2-inch lengths*

2 *tablespoons toasted sesame seeds*

Skin and bone the chicken breasts and cut into small pieces. (*See page 94 for instructions on boning chicken breasts.*) Cut the cauliflower and broccoli florets into bite-sized pieces. Peel the broccoli stems' tough outer skin; quarter the stalk lengthwise and cut into 2-inch pieces. Prepare the carrots, bell pepper and green onions. Heat 1 tablespoon oil in a large, heavy skillet or wok over medium high heat. When the oil is hot, stir in the garlic, pepper flakes and ginger. Add the chicken to the skillet and stir-fry until the meat turns white. Add 1 teaspoon bean paste softened in a small amount of warm water, and stir to coat the chicken. Remove from the skillet.

Add 1 tablespoon of oil to the skillet. Stir in the cauliflower, broccoli, carrots and bell pepper. Add 1 teaspoon bean paste stirred smooth in 3 tablespoons warm water. Coat the vegetables with the oil and bean paste. Cover the pan for 1 minute. Remove the lid and stir-fry for 2 minutes. Add 1 ¾ cup chicken stock; cover and bring to boil. Check the broccoli and cauliflower; you want them not quite tender. Stir the cornstarch and remaining broth until smooth and add it to the vegetables. Stir in the chicken and continue cooking until the sauce thickens slightly. Serve over rice and garnish. If you are serving noodles, stir them in with the chicken to reheat.

HOT SAUSAGE VARIATION

Omit the chicken and dried red pepper flakes. Poach 2 hot Italian sausages, poking them all over with a fork to reduce their fat content. (You can keep the sausages on hand in the freezer and poach them frozen.) Remove the sausage casings and chop well. Stir into the vegetables when they are not quite tender-crisp. The fennel in some Italian sausages adds a very nice flavor.

Middle Eastern Salad
Zucchini Pancakes

SERVES 4

TIME TO PREPARE

30 minutes

INGREDIENTS

ON HAND

- ☐ *2 cups cooked chicken or turkey (optional)*
- ☐ *4 eggs*
- ☐ *unbleached or whole wheat flour*
- ☐ *4 tablespoons sesame seeds (preferably unhulled)*
- ☐ *mayonnaise*
- ☐ *vegetable oil*
- ☐ *fresh garlic*
- ☐ *ground cumin*
- ☐ *turmeric*
- ☐ *oregano*
- ☐ *baking powder*

SHOPPING LIST

- ☐ *8 small zucchini*
- ☐ *24 cherry tomatoes or ½ lb. fresh mushrooms*
- ☐ *2 red bell peppers*
- ☐ *2 green bell peppers*
- ☐ *1 large yellow onion*
- ☐ *6 large green onions*
- ☐ *2 15-oz. cans garbanzo beans*
- ☐ *1 can pitted black olives (5 ¾-oz. drained)*
- ☐ *8 oz. plain low-fat yogurt*

This bean salad always gets rave reviews but takes just 15 minutes to assemble. Because it doesn't suffer from being mixed ahead of time, it is ideal to take on a picnic or to a potluck, but be careful to keep it cool because it has mayonnaise in it. If red peppers are unavailable, use all green peppers. When peppers are out of season, try rehydrating dried red and green peppers; they are surprisingly tasty. This bean salad is equally good with or without the addition of chicken or turkey. Served with spears of crisp cucumber and interestingly textured bread or crackers, it is a well-balanced meal in itself.

Garbanzo beans grow two to a pod like peas, they are sometimes called chick peas, but they are not peas. In Italy, garbanzo beans are called *ceci* (pronounced tchay-tchee), a word which played a peculiar role in Italian history. It was chosen by the Sicilians rebelling against Charles I of Anjou in 1282 to ferret out the French. Anyone who couldn't correctly pronounce "ceci" was killed.

OVERVIEW

1. Put a platter in the oven to warm.

2. Make the salad dressing and refrigerate it.

3. Prepare the zucchini batter. As the pancakes fry, prepare the salad ingredients and put them into a bowl. As they finish cooking, transfer the pancakes into a warm oven.

4. Dress the salad and serve on individual lettuce-lined plates. Serve the pancakes on the warmed platter; they can be eaten out of hand like bread.

Zucchini Pancakes

vegetable oil

4 cups coarsely grated zucchini

½ cup coarsely grated onion

4 large eggs, beaten lightly (or 8 egg whites, if you are concerned about cholesterol)

1 cup unbleached or whole wheat flour

4 tablespoons sesame seeds (preferably unhulled)

1 teaspoon baking powder

1 teaspoon salt

½ teaspoon dried oregano

Stir together the grated zucchini, onion and eggs. Mix together the dry ingredients and stir into the zucchini mixture. Heat just enough oil to coat the surface of a skillet (or use a nonstick pan). Spoon the batter onto the cooking surface and brown on each side. (Cook the pancakes over medium heat so that they cook all the way through before browning.) Transfer the cooked pancakes to a platter in the oven. Loosely cover them with foil so that they don't dry out.

Middle Eastern Salad

DRESSING

¼ cup mayonnaise

1 cup plain low-fat yogurt

2 cloves garlic, pressed

1 teaspoon ground cumin

⅛ teaspoon turmeric

freshly ground pepper and salt to taste

2 15-oz. cans of garbanzo beans, drained and rinsed

1 cup sliced pitted black olives

6 large green onions, finely sliced, fresh stem included

2 green peppers, coarsely diced

2 red peppers, coarsely diced

24 cherry tomatoes, halved or ½ lb. small mushrooms, steamed 5 minutes and cooled

2 cups shredded cooked chicken or julienned turkey slices (optional)

Combine dressing ingredients. Refrigerate covered; it is quite odoriferous. Prepare the salad ingredients. Toss together with the dressing just before serving. Serve on individual plates lined with lettuce leaves.

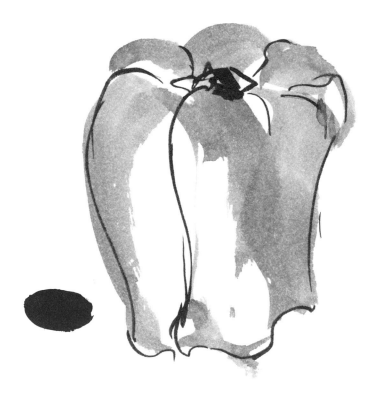

Bourbon Chicken with Walnuts

Parsley Carrots

Rice

SERVES 4

TIME TO PREPARE

30 minutes

INGREDIENTS

ON HAND
- [ ] *1 egg*
- [ ] *cornstarch*
- [ ] *soy sauce*
- [ ] *bourbon*
- [ ] *sugar*
- [ ] *fresh garlic*
- [ ] *fresh ginger*
- [ ] *vegetable oil*
- [ ] *brown rice*

SHOPPING LIST
- [ ] *2 whole chicken breasts*
- [ ] *¾ cup shelled and broken walnuts*
- [ ] *8 green onions*
- [ ] *4 carrots*
- [ ] *fresh parsley*

This is an unusual variation of the basic stir-fry. The walnuts make the meal rich and filling; what may not appear to be a large amount of food on the plate will satisfy even the biggest appetites.

Today we include nuts in our diet as an embellishment rather than as a staple. In earlier times, nuts were a crucially important high calorie food that could be gathered and stored through the winter. Intensive cultivation of walnuts occurred as early as the 4th century in France's Grenoble region (which still produces the finest walnuts in France and perhaps the world). Walnuts were the principal food of the poor in medieval times in France's Dordogne region, and in 15th century Paris walnuts were sometimes the only food available at the market. Walnut meat was blanched, pulverized and soaked in water to provide the standard "milk" in many households until the end of the 18th century.

OVERVIEW

1. If you precooked rice in the morning, complete cooking the rice now. With precooked rice (*see page 99 for directions*) this meal will take 30 minutes to cook. If you are starting rice from scratch it will take 45 to 50 minutes.

2. Complete preparations for the carrots, but don't begin cooking them.

3. Prepare the ingredients for the chicken dish. Before you begin to stir-fry, start cooking the carrots.

Parsley Carrots

4 medium-sized carrots, sliced
   thin on the diagonal

2 tablespoons water and a dribble
   of oil (sesame or light vegetable)

2 tablespoons minced fresh parsley

In a tightly covered, heavy saucepan, cook the carrots over medium heat. The carrots will be tender in approximately 5 to 7 minutes. Check three-quarters of the way through cooking to make sure they are not about to be scorched. Mince and stir in parsley just before serving.

Bourbon Chicken with Walnuts

2 whole chicken breasts

1 egg (if you are concerned about
   cholesterol, use only the egg
   white)

1 teaspoon cornstarch

1 tablespoon water or chicken stock

1 tablespoon bourbon

½ teaspoon sugar

3 tablespoons soy sauce

8 green onions cut into 2-inch
   lengths, stems included

1 clove garlic, minced

2 slices fresh ginger, minced

¾ cup shelled and broken walnut
   meat

2 tablespoons vegetable oil

Skin and bone the chicken; cut into bite-sized pieces. (*See page 94 for instructions.*) Mix together the next 3 ingredients and stir the chicken pieces in this mixture. Combine the bourbon, sugar and soy sauce. Heat the oil in a heavy skillet or wok. Stir-fry the chicken until it turns white (about 3 to 5 minutes). Remove from skillet. Stir-fry the green onions, garlic and ginger, adding a tablespoon or 2 of water to keep them from sticking to the pan. Cook 1 minute. Add the bourbon mixture, chicken, and walnuts. Heat thoroughly and serve.

Kitsune Soba (Fox Noodles)

SERVES 4

TIME TO PREPARE

*60 minutes the first few times;
30 minutes once you learn how*

INGREDIENTS

ON HAND

☐ *sugar*

☐ *soy sauce*

☐ *Tabasco (optional)*

SHOPPING LIST

☐ *1 whole chicken breast*

☐ *1 bunch of greens (kale, mustard, spinach, chard, etc.)*

☐ *3 green onions*

☐ *1 lb. soba (buckwheat noodles) or 1 lb. spaghetti*

☐ *6 dried mushrooms*

☐ *6 pieces aburage*

☐ *mirin*

☐ *To Make Dashi:*

☐ *½ oz. kombu*

☐ *½ oz. hanagatsuo*

Every Japanese cookbook seems to have its own story about why this dish is called Fox Noodles. In Japanese folktales, the fox is an evil, magical spirit known to be fond of fried bean curd. This Osaka version of Kitsune Soba, a bean curd and buckwheat noodle soup, has chicken in it, too, to doubly delight the fox in you.

Many of the ingredients in this recipe may be unfamiliar to you, but they are all available in Asian markets or gourmet shops and possibly at your local supermarket. *Aburage*, or fried bean curd, is spongey and deep-fried—not at all like fried cubes of tofu. *Soba* are buckwheat noodles, a hearty, pleasant change from wheat, but any noodles will do. *Mirin* is sweet Japanese rice wine used only in cooking.

Dashi is the broth that forms the basis for nearly every Japanese soup. Instant dashi is available to which you add only water, but all brands include MSG (as does the traditional recipe), so I prefer to make my own. Dashi is made by boiling shaved dried bonito (*hanagatsuo*) with kelp (*kombu*) in water. Do not purchase *katsuobushi*, which is a piece of dried bonito fillet; you need a special tool to shave it.

Once you make this recipe, you will see that it is a wonderful, basic method of preparation. You could substitute sturdy fish fillets such as rock fish or snapper, or shellfish, or tofu, for the chicken. A variety of vegetables could be added.

OVERVIEW

1. Soak dried mushrooms.

2. Prepare kakejiru broth.

3. Prepare noodles. When they are *al dente*, drain, rinse and set aside.

4. Dip the aburage in the boiling water as the noodles cook to remove the excess oil.

5. Prepare aburage mixture.

6. Combine aburage mixture and kakejiru broth. Cook chicken and vegetables.

7. Assemble and serve.

Dashi (Basic Soup Stock)

10 minutes to prepare

6 cups water

½ oz. hanagatsuo

½ oz. kombu

Bring the water to a boil. Add kombu and boil 3 to 4 minutes. Stir occasionally. Remove kombu and stir in bonito shavings. Bring broth to boil; remove from heat. Allow the bonito to settle to the bottom of the pot. Strain.

Chicken stock may be substituted for dashi. Grate a 2-inch piece of ginger into 2 quarts of chicken stock and bring to a boil. Simmer for 5 minutes and strain.

Kitsune Soba

6 dried mushrooms

KAKEJIRU BROTH

6 cups dashi (see recipe above)

½ cup mirin

½ cup light soy sauce or 2 tablespoons water and 4 tablespoons soy sauce

1 lb. soba (buckwheat noodles) or spaghetti, broken into 3-inch lengths

6 pieces aburage

4 tablespoons soy sauce

2 tablespoons mirin

1 tablespoon sugar

1 whole chicken breast, or ¾ lb. boned cooked chicken

1 bunch of greens (kale, chard, mustard, spinach)

3 green onions

Soak the dried mushrooms in just enough warm water to barely cover them.

Prepare the kakejiru broth: bring the dashi to a boil; add ½ cup mirin and ½ cup light soy sauce (or 2 tablespoons water and 4 tablespoons soy sauce). Simmer 10 minutes.

Cook the noodles. While the water is boiling, dip in the 6 pieces of aburage to remove the excess oil. Place the aburage between paper towels to absorb the water. When the noodles are *al dente*, drain in colander and rinse under cold running water. Set aside.

In a saucepan, stir together 4 tablespoons soy sauce, 2 tablespoons mirin, and 1 tablespoon sugar. Drain the mushrooms (save the water for stock). Discard the hard stems and slice the caps into ¼-inch pieces. Add to the saucepan. Gently squeeze dry the aburage in paper towels and cut into ½-inch pieces; stir into the saucepan and simmer until the liquid is absorbed by the aburage. Set aside.

Begin boiling water to reheat noodles. Bone and skin the chicken and cut into bite-sized pieces. (*See page 94 for instructions.*) Slice 3 green onions on the diagonal into ½-inch pieces. Wash and coarsely chop the chard, kale or other greens. Bring the kakejiru broth to a boil. If the chicken is uncooked, simmer in the kakejiru broth for 5 minutes. Add the greens, but not the onions. (If you are using cooked chicken or substituting fish, stir it in now.)

Warm the noodles by pouring the pot of boiling water over them. Drain well. Now add the green onions to the soup. Divide the warm noodles amongst four large, warm soup bowls. Ladle the aburage mixture over the noodles, then the soup. Serve immediately. You may want to add a shot of hot pepper. The appropriate Japanese pepper is called *shichimi*, but Tabasco will do.

Chinese Chicken Noodle Soup
Ginger Sesame Cucumber Salad

SERVES 4

(easily halved)

TIME TO PREPARE

30 minutes

INGREDIENTS

ON HAND

☐ *soy sauce*
☐ *dry sherry*
☐ *4 oz. noodles*
☐ *1 egg*
☐ *2 quarts chicken stock*
☐ *vegetable oil*
☐ *sesame seeds (2 teaspoons)*
☐ *fresh garlic*
☐ *honey*
☐ *white vinegar*
☐ *ground ginger*

SHOPPING LIST

☐ *2 green onions*
☐ *1 whole chicken breast (or 1 cup cooked chicken on hand)*
☐ *1 bunch fresh spinach or other greens (chard, kale, etc.)*
☐ *2 large, firm cucumbers*

This meal is so easy to make yet good tasting and nurturing that it may become one of your tired evening standards. Alter the soup's ingredients to include what's available in your refrigerator or garden. Substitute any greens (chard, mustard, kale, or collard, for example) for the spinach. One or two cups of diced tofu could be substituted for or added to the chicken. Use soft tofu in soups. Firm tofu is best in stir-fried dishes or marinaded in salads.

OVERVIEW

1. Begin to bring chicken stock to a boil. Prepare the cucumber salad. Add the noodles to the boiling stock.

2. Finish preparing the soup.

Chinese Chicken Noodle Soup

2 quarts chicken stock

1 cup cooked chicken or 1 whole
  chicken breast

4 oz. noodles

1 bunch spinach

2 green onions

3 tablespoons soy sauce

1 tablespoon dry sherry

1 teaspoon salt

1 egg, lightly beaten

Bring the stock to a boil. Bone the chicken breast; skin and cut into bite-sized pieces. (*See page 94 for instructions.*) Add the noodles to the boiling stock. Bring to a second boil and simmer until the noodles are *al dente*.

As the noodles cook, rinse the spinach well; remove tough stems and coarsely chop. Trim the green onions; shred them lengthwise and then cut crosswise into 1-inch lengths. When the noodles are cooked *al dente*, stir the uncooked chicken, soy sauce, sherry and salt into the stock. When the chicken is no longer pink, add the spinach. If you are using cooked chicken, add it to the soup pot along with the spinach.

Bring the soup to a boil. Slowly stir in the egg. Ladle the soup into large bowls. Garnish with green onions and serve.

Ginger Sesame Cucumber Salad

2 large firm cucumbers

2 tablespoons vegetable oil

2 teaspoons sesame seeds

1 clove garlic, peeled and
  quartered

1 tablespoon honey

2 tablespoons white vinegar

1 tablespoon dry sherry

1/8 teaspoon ground ginger

1/4 teaspoon salt

Peel the cucumbers if the skin is bitter, tough or waxed. Cut them in half lengthwise, remove seeds and slice the cucumbers as thin as possible. In a small saucepan, stir the oil, sesame seeds and garlic over medium heat until the seeds are toasted. Remove from heat; discard the garlic. Add the honey and stir smooth. Stir in all the remaining ingredients except for the cucumbers. Place the cucumbers in a bowl and toss with the dressing. Cover and chill until serving.

Baked Chicken Legs with Ginger/Fennel Orange Sauce

Lemon, Ginger and Raisin Relish

Sesame-Garlic Kasha

Szechuan-Style Green Beans

SERVES 2

(easily doubled)

TIME TO PREPARE

40 minutes

INGREDIENTS

ON HAND

☐ *1 egg*
☐ *1 green onion*
☐ *vegetable oil*
☐ *sesame oil*
☐ *raisins*
☐ *honey*
☐ *rice vinegar*
☐ *soy sauce*
☐ *Tabasco*
☐ *fresh garlic*
☐ *fresh ginger*
☐ *fennel seeds (or anise)*
☐ *ground ginger*
☐ *cornstarch*

SHOPPING LIST

☐ *4 to 6 chicken legs*
☐ *1 6-oz. can frozen orange juice*
☐ *¾ cup kasha*
☐ *½ lb. fresh green beans*
☐ *1 lemon*

Kasha is roasted buckwheat groats. It is available in bulk at health food stores, and can also be found packaged in supermarkets.

OVERVIEW

1. Preheat oven to 325°. Prepare the Ginger and Fennel Orange Sauce, peeling an additional garlic clove for the kasha.

2. While the orange sauce simmers, prepare the chicken for baking and the Raisin Relish (mincing an extra tablespoon of ginger for the green bean dish).

3. Begin baking the chicken.

4. Prepare the ingredients for the green beans. Set aside.

5. Prepare the kasha.

6. Ten minutes before the chicken finishes baking, begin to cook the green beans.

7. The kasha, green beans and chicken should finish cooking at the same time. Serve at once.

Lemon, Ginger and Raisin Relish

½ cup raisins

juice of 1 lemon

½ tablespoon minced fresh ginger

2 tablespoons water

Blend ingredients together in a food processor or blender. This relish is too simple to taste so good. Excellent alongside an Indian curry dish.

Baked Chicken Legs with Ginger/Fennel Orange Sauce

4 to 6 chicken legs

GINGER AND FENNEL
ORANGE SAUCE

1 6-oz. can frozen orange juice

¾ cup water

2 tablespoons vegetable oil

2 cloves garlic, pressed

2 teaspoons fennel seeds or anise

½ teaspoon ground ginger

1 teaspoon salt

lots of freshly ground pepper

1 tablespoon cornstarch mixed
   with 1 tablespoon water

Preheat the oven to 325°. In a saucepan, bring to a boil all the sauce's ingredients except for the cornstarch mixture. Simmer 5 minutes; stir the cornstarch and water into the sauce. Continue stirring until slightly thickened, or about 1 minute. Remove from heat.

Lavish the sauce on all sides of the drumsticks. Bake for 30 minutes, turning them over halfway through baking time and spooning over them the sauce that has dripped into the baking dish.

The leftover orange sauce can be stored in the refrigerator for 2 weeks, or frozen. Pop it out of the freezer container and reheat when you are ready to use it. This sauce is also good brushed on pork chops.

Sesame Garlic Kasha

¾ cup kasha

1 tablespoon sesame oil

1 egg, lightly beaten

1 ¾ cups boiling water

1 tablespoon soy sauce

1 clove garlic, pressed

Sauté the kasha in the sesame oil until you can smell it roasting. Pour in the egg and continue stirring until the egg is cooked and the grains of kasha are separate. Stir in the boiling water and simmer uncovered 3 minutes. Stir in the garlic and soy sauce; cover and cook over very low heat 10 minutes. Remove from heat. Let sit 5 minutes, or until you are ready to serve.

Szechuan-Style Green Beans

½ lb. fresh green beans, sliced into
   1¼-inch lengths

1 tablespoon sesame oil

1 tablespoon minced fresh ginger

1 tablespoon rice vinegar

1 tablespoon honey

1 tablespoon soy sauce

2 tablespoons thinly sliced green
   onion

a few drops Tabasco

Heat the oil in a frying pan that has a lid, or in a wok. When you can smell the oil's nutty fragrance, stir in the ginger for 30 seconds; remove the pan from the heat. Stir in the remaining ingredients except for the Tabasco sauce and sliced green onion. Return the pan to the heat, cover and simmer 7 minutes, or until the beans are tender-crisp. Just before serving, stir in the green onion and a few drops of Tabasco sauce.

Roasted Chicken with Chili and Garlic

Hashed Brown Potatoes

Sautéed Cabbage

SERVES 4

TIME TO PREPARE

60 minutes

INGREDIENTS

ON HAND
- ☐ *dry sherry or dry white wine*
- ☐ *vegetable oil*
- ☐ *fresh garlic*
- ☐ *chili powder*

SHOPPING LIST
- ☐ *1 3-lb. chicken*
- ☐ *4 medium-sized red potatoes*
- ☐ *1 green bell pepper*
- ☐ *1 head of cabbage*
- ☐ *1 lemon*
- ☐ *fresh chives*

Baking a chicken is certainly one of the easiest solutions for a tired cook. This rendition repeats what began as a delicious mistake— rubbing the bird with chili powder rather than paprika. A layer of thinly sliced lemons atop the baking bird keeps it moist without additional butter or oil, or basting.

You'll find the humble cabbage honored here. This generally neglected vegetable is cheap, available year round, and can be stored for a long time in the refrigerator with little ill effect. It is equally tasty raw in a salad or cooked.

OVERVIEW

1. Preheat the oven to 350°. Prepare the chicken according to recipe below.

2. Twenty-five minutes before the chicken is finished baking, begin to prepare the potatoes.

3. When the potatoes finish cooking, you should be able to remove the chicken from the oven, turn the oven off, and put the potatoes into a bowl and in the oven to keep warm. Use the same frying pan used to cook the potatoes to sauté the cabbage. Set the table, carve the chicken, serve the chicken and potatoes on warm plates, and the cabbage should be ready to serve.

Roasted Chicken with Chili and Garlic

1 3-lb. whole fryer

3 to 4 cloves garlic, pressed

1 tablespoon chili powder

1 large lemon, thinly sliced

Preheat the oven to 350°. Rinse the chicken in cold water. Place it breast side up in a baking pan and pat dry with paper towels. Rub the chicken all over with pressed garlic and chili powder. Cover the legs and breast of the chicken with slices of lemon. Bake for 60 minutes. Slice between the thigh and body and probe the flesh for doneness. If the juice runs pink, let the chicken bake a few minutes longer.

Hashed Brown Potatoes

4 medium-sized red potatoes

1 green bell pepper

1 tablespoon vegetable oil

¼ to ½ teaspoon salt

3 tablespoons minced fresh chives

Scrub the potatoes clean. Dice into ⅓-inch cubes. Coarsely dice the green pepper. Heat the oil in a heavy skillet; stir in the potatoes, green pepper, and salt, coating the vegetables with the oil. Cover. Cook over medium heat, stirring every 5 minutes or so, making sure the potatoes aren't burning or sticking to the pan. When the potatoes are soft, stir in the chives.

Sautéed Cabbage

½ head cabbage, thinly sliced (a food processor makes this very easy)

1 tablespoon vegetable oil

2 tablespoons dry sherry or dry white wine

salt to taste

Heat the oil in a large frying pan over medium heat. Stir in the cabbage and wine. Lightly sprinkle with salt and stir. Cover and cook until barely tender, or about 3 minutes.

Boned Breast of Chicken with White Wine and Tarragon

Noodles and Chopped Black Olives

Baked Herbed Stuffed Tomatoes

SERVES 2

TIME TO PREPARE

35 minutes

INGREDIENTS

ON HAND
- ☐ *egg noodles (4 to 6 oz.)*
- ☐ *olive oil*
- ☐ *light vegetable oil*
- ☐ *butter*
- ☐ *1 slice bread*
- ☐ *arrowroot or cornstarch*
- ☐ *flour*
- ☐ *fresh garlic*
- ☐ *2 green onions*
- ☐ *thyme*
- ☐ *basil*
- ☐ *tarragon*
- ☐ *Parmesan cheese*

SHOPPING LIST
- ☐ *2 chicken breast halves*
- ☐ *1 can pitted black olives (5-¾ oz. drained)*
- ☐ *2 large ripe tomatoes*
- ☐ *fresh parsley*

This method of cooking boned chicken breasts is a basic, foolproof method which frees you from the anxiety of overcooking, and therefore rendering stringy and tough, the potentially succulent, tender breast. Using this technique, exact timing is not necessary. (You cannot, however, use unthawed, frozen chicken breasts.)

What you decide to do with this moist fillet is limited only by your imagination. This recipe dresses the chicken in a classic sauce of white wine and tarragon, but why not try mushrooms and Madeira, or chopped peanuts, honey and soy, or marinara and melted Jack cheese, or . . .

OVERVIEW

1. Preheat oven to 350°. Prepare and begin to bake tomatoes. Peel an extra clove of garlic for the noodles.

2. Prepare and begin to cook the chicken breasts.

3. Boil water to cook the noodles. Chop the black olives; grate the Parmesan cheese.

4. Warm a platter in the oven to hold the cooked chicken breasts. When the breasts are done, transfer them to the platter and make the wine sauce in the skillet. As the sauce simmers, toss the noodles with the olive oil, olives and garlic.

5. Serve the noodles on warm plates. Lay a chicken breast on top and ladle the sauce over the chicken and noodles. Sprinkle with Parmesan. Remove the tomatoes from the oven; gently transfer them to the plates with a spatula.

Baked Herbed Stuffed Tomatoes

2 large ripe tomatoes

2 tablespoons chopped parsley

2 tablespoons chopped green onions

1 clove garlic, pressed

⅛ teaspoon thyme

2 tablespoons fresh basil or ¾ tablespoon dried basil

¼ cup bread crumbs

1 teaspoon olive oil

Preheat oven to 350°. Slice off the top of the tomatoes and scoop the innards into a chopping bowl. Add herbs, green onion and garlic and finely chop all the ingredients. Stir in the bread crumbs and olive oil. Spoon this mixture into the tomatoes; replace each tomato's "lid." Bake for 30 minutes. Transfer to the serving plate with a spatula.

Boned Breast of Chicken with White Wine and Tarragon

2 chicken breast halves

flour

½ tablespoon butter

½ tablespoon light vegetable oil

½ cup dry white wine

1 teaspoon dried tarragon or 2 teaspoons fresh tarragon

1 teaspoon arrowroot or cornstarch

Skin and bone the breasts. (*See page 94 for instructions.*) Heat the butter and oil in a heavy skillet with a lid. Dredge the chicken in flour. Put the breasts in hot oil; cover the skillet and reduce the heat to very low. After 10 minutes, turn the meat over and cook in the same manner for another 10 minutes. Remove the skillet from the heat and let the breasts sit in the covered skillet 10 minutes longer.

Just before serving, place the breasts on a warm plate. Heat the skillet over medium heat and add the wine, tarragon and arrowroot. Stir until the sauce thickens. Spoon over the chicken and noodles.

Noodles and Chopped Black Olives

4 to 6 oz. egg noodles

1 clove garlic, pressed

1 teaspoon olive oil

½ to ¾ cup chopped black olives

3 tablespoons freshly grated Parmesan cheese

Cook noodles *al dente*. Rinse under hot running water; drain well. Toss with garlic, olive oil and chopped black olives. Season with salt and pepper. Sprinkle Parmesan cheese over the noodles and chicken.

FISH DISHES

Red Snapper with Herbed Tomatoes and Guacamole

Corn on the Cob (or Cornbread)

Chilled Slices of Jicama

Butter Lettuce in Vinaigrette Dressing

SERVES 4

TIME TO PREPARE

50 minutes

INGREDIENTS

ON HAND
- ☐ *olive oil*
- ☐ *vegetable oil*
- ☐ *wine vinegar or 1 lemon*
- ☐ *cornmeal or flour*
- ☐ *fresh garlic*
- ☐ *fresh or dried herbs (parsley, thyme, chervil and/or oregano)*
- ☐ *Tabasco*

  Following ingredients are for optional cornbread:
- ☐ *yellow cornmeal (1 ½ cups)*
- ☐ *flour*
- ☐ *baking soda*
- ☐ *milk (¾ to 1 cup)*
- ☐ *butter*
- ☐ *1 egg*
- ☐ *honey or sugar*

  SHOPPING LIST
- ☐ *1 ½ lbs. red snapper fillets*
- ☐ *1 16-oz. can whole peeled tomatoes*
- ☐ *1 ripe avocado*
- ☐ *1 lime*
- ☐ *3 shallots*
- ☐ *1 jicama*
- ☐ *4 ears fresh corn*
- ☐ *butter lettuce*

When fresh corn is not available, cornbread makes a good substitute. The Seneca tribe of the Iroquois Federation believed that corn came from Sky Woman's daughter who was buried on Earth when she died. Potatoes vined out from her toes, from her fingers beans sprang, squash plants wended their way from her abdomen, and from her breasts sprouted corn.

OVERVIEW

1. Preheat the oven to 350°. If you are making cornbread, mix together the ingredients, pour into an oiled pan and put into the oven.

2. Prepare the snapper. Bake for 25 minutes.

3. If you are preparing corn, prepare it for steaming, but don't begin cooking it until 5 minutes before the fish is done.

4. Prepare the salad dressing and greens. (*See page 100 for Vinaigrette Dressings.*) Cover and chill the salad greens until ready to toss with dressing and serve.

5. Peel and slice the jicama; sprinkle with fresh lime juice. Cover and chill until serving.

6. Prepare the guacamole. Toss the salad. Serve.

Chilled Slices of Jicama

If you have never tried jicama, you are in for a treat. It is a crunchy, sweet bulbous root vegetable from Mexico that is eaten raw. Peel it (the skin is easy to pare) and cut into thin slices as you would an apple. Squeeze fresh lime juice over it, cover and chill until serving.

Cornbread (optional)

½ cup whole wheat or white flour

1 ½ cups yellow cornmeal

½ teaspoon baking soda

½ teaspoon salt

4 tablespoons honey or sugar

¼ cup melted butter (½ stick)

¾ cup milk (1 cup if using sugar)

1 egg

Preheat oven to 350°. Mix together the dry ingredients. Stir the honey or sugar into the melted butter. When combined thoroughly, stir in the milk and egg. Add the liquid ingredients to the dry mixture. Combine thoroughly but gently. Pour into an oiled, shallow 9-inch square pan. Bake at 350° for 30 minutes, or until done.

Steamed Corn on the Cob

Husk the corn and pile into a steamer set in a pot of water. Cover tightly. The corn will take about 5 minutes to cook after the water starts to boil. Pierce a kernel with the tip of a knife to see if the corn is tender.

Red Snapper with Herbed Tomatoes and Guacamole

1 ½ lbs. red snapper fillets

cornmeal or flour for dredging

3 tablespoons olive oil

3 shallots, minced

3 cloves garlic, minced

1 16-oz. can whole peeled tomatoes, drained

1 tablespoon fresh chopped herbs (a mixture of thyme, parsley, chervil and/or oregano) or 1 ½ teaspoons dried herbs

GUACAMOLE

1 ripe avocado

1 clove garlic, minced

1 to 2 teaspoons fresh lime juice

Tabasco or other hot red pepper sauce

salt and pepper to taste

Preheat the oven to 350°. Rinse the fish in cold water and pat dry. Salt and pepper the fish, then dredge it in cornmeal or flour. Shake off any excess. Heat 3 tablespoons olive oil in a large, heavy skillet and fry the fillets over high heat. Cook 2 to 3 minutes on each side, depending upon thickness. With a spatula, carefully move the fish to a baking dish large enough to lay the fillets flat.

In the same skillet, sauté the shallots and garlic over a medium heat. When they are golden, add the tomatoes, breaking them up in the skillet with a large metal spoon or spatula. Cook for 2 minutes. Spoon the mixture evenly over the fish. Sprinkle with the herbs. Lay a buttered piece of waxed paper over the fish and bake for 25 minutes.

Just before taking the fish out of the oven, prepare the guacamole: fork-mash the avocado with lime juice, a pressed clove of garlic, salt, pepper and Tabasco to taste. Serve the fish on warm plates. Spoon some guacamole on each serving. Garnish with lime slices.

Butter Lettuce in Vinaigrette Dressing
See page 100 for instructions.

Fillets of Fish Poached in Spiced Buttermilk

Orange Peel Pilaf

Sautéed Broccoli with Lemon

SERVES 3

TIME TO PREPARE

40 minutes

INGREDIENTS

ON HAND
- [ ] *cracked wheat or bulgur*
- [ ] *Chinese sesame oil or vegetable oil*
- [ ] *butter*
- [ ] *turmeric*
- [ ] *cumin seed*
- [ ] *⅓ cup raisins*

SHOPPING LIST
- [ ] *1 ½ lbs. fish (fillets of halibut, haddock, rock cod, red snapper)*
- [ ] *1 quart buttermilk*
- [ ] *2 lemons*
- [ ] *1 orange*
- [ ] *1 small yellow onion*
- [ ] *1 bunch broccoli*
- [ ] *⅓ cup chopped peanuts (dry roasted and unsalted) or slivered or chopped almonds*
- [ ] *⅓ cup raisins*

Here is an exotic but simple way to prepare any firm, light-fleshed fish. Lemon and buttermilk bring out the clean, sweet taste of fresh fish while the spices provide a subtle background flavor. The fish and sauce are brilliant yellow (from the turmeric), which is striking next to the confetti-like Orange Peel Pilaf and deep broccoli green.

OVERVIEW

1. Prepare the fish for cooking.

2. Begin cooking the pilaf.

3. Poach the fish in the buttermilk 5 minutes. As it poaches, quarter a lemon; wash and cut up the broccoli.

4. Remove the fish to a platter. Reduce poaching liquid; return the fish to the pan and simmer uncovered 5 to 10 minutes.

5. During the last 5 minutes of simmering the fish, sauté the broccoli. Move the fish to a warm platter and set in the oven. Further reduce the poaching liquid until it is thick enough to sauce the fish. Serve.

Orange Peel Pilaf

⅓ cup raisins

⅓ cup chopped dry roasted
    unsalted peanuts or chopped or
    slivered almonds

the juice and grated rind of 1
    orange, preferably organic (or
    substitute the juice of 1 orange
    plus ¼ cup minced dried
    apricots)

¾ cup cracked wheat or bulgur

1 small yellow onion, chopped

1 tablespoon oil, preferably
    Chinese sesame oil

1 ½ cups water

Put the raisins, nuts, orange juice and orange rind into a blender and whirl together for 2 seconds. Over medium high heat, sauté the wheat and chopped onion in 1 tablespoon oil until the wheat is toasted, or about 3 minutes. Reduce the heat and add the water and the orange mixture. Cover and cook over very low heat for 15 to 20 minutes. When the wheat is cooked, fluff with a fork, cock the lid of the pot slightly and keep in a warm oven until the fish and broccoli are ready to serve.

Fillets Poached in Spiced Buttermilk

1 ½ lbs. fillets of firm, light–
    fleshed fish (rock cod, halibut,
    snapper, or haddock)

¾ teaspoon turmeric

freshly ground black pepper to taste

3 cups buttermilk

½ tablespoon lemon juice

½ teaspoon salt

2 teaspoons cumin seed

Rinse the fish in cold water and pat dry with paper towels. Rub with turmeric and black pepper. In a large heavy skillet, poach the fish in the buttermilk for 5 minutes. (The buttermilk will curdle. Don't fret.) Remove the fish and add the lemon juice and salt. Reduce the cooking liquid by one-half over high heat. Add the cumin seed, reduce the heat and return the fish to the skillet. Simmer uncovered until the fish is just barely flakey, or about 5 to 10 minutes.

Carefully move the fish to a warm plate and place in a warm oven. Reduce the cooking liquid over a high heat until it is a sauce you can ladle over the fish.

Sautéed Broccoli with Lemon

1 bunch broccoli

3 tablespoons water plus 1
    tablespoon butter

lemon juice to taste (about 2
    tablespoons)

To prepare the broccoli, cut off and divide the flowerets. Cut off the ends of the stalks and peel away their tough outer skin. Cut into 2-inch lengths and quarter each piece. In a heavy skillet or wok, heat the butter and water until the butter melts. Stir in the broccoli; cover and cook over medium high heat for 3 to 4 minutes. Check. Is the broccoli tender-crisp? Does the pan need more water? When the broccoli is to your liking, sprinkle with lemon juice, toss and serve.

Pan Poached Fish with Green Onions or Shallots

New Potatoes with Parsley

Spinach, Red Onion, Avocado and Orange Salad with Sherry Dressing

SERVES 2

TIME TO PREPARE

30 minutes

INGREDIENTS

ON HAND

☐ *chicken stock or dry white wine (½ cup)*

☐ *butter*

☐ *olive oil*

☐ *dry sherry*

☐ *white vinegar*

☐ *fresh garlic*

☐ *curry powder*

SHOPPING LIST

☐ *¾ lb. fish (fillets or steaks) or 1 small dressed fish up to 1 ½ inches thick*

☐ *3 green onions or 2 shallots*

☐ *1 small red onion*

☐ *fresh parsley*

☐ *8 golf ball-sized new potatoes*

☐ *1 bunch fresh spinach*

☐ *1 navel orange*

☐ *1 ripe avocado*

☐ *1 lemon (optional)*

You can use fresh or frozen fish in this recipe. Frozen fish retains its juices and texture much better if cooked frozen. If you must thaw fish, do so in the refrigerator.

A friend of mine hikes every summer to the same isolated mountain lake. There he cooks over an open fire the trout he has caught, first stuffing it with wild onions. This is similar to the way fish is prepared in the recipe below, and it's not very different from the way people have been cooking fish for the last several thousand years.

OVERVIEW

1. Prepare the salad dressing and salad makings—all except for the avocado. Cover and chill the salad until ready to toss and serve.

2. Scrub the potatoes. Begin to steam them.

3. Mince the green onions or shallots; mince the parsley. Peel the garlic and set it in the press.

4. Put a platter in the oven to warm.

5. Rinse the fish in cold water and pat dry. Begin cooking it. As it simmers, slice the avocado into the salad, dress and toss.

6. Remove the cooked fish to a warm platter. As you reduce the poaching liquid, toss the potatoes with butter and parsley; season with salt and pepper.

Spinach, Red Onion, Avocado and Orange Salad with Sherry Dressing

1 bunch fresh spinach

1 small red onion, very thinly sliced

1 navel orange, peeled, halved and sectioned

1 ripe avocado

Prepare the Sherry Dressing (*see page 103*). Rinse and dry the spinach; remove tough stems and tear the leaves into a salad bowl. Add the onions and orange; cover and chill until just before serving. Slice the avocado into the salad. Dress and toss. This salad responds well to a few extra twists of the pepper grinder.

New Potatoes with Parsley

8 very small new potatoes, scrubbed clean

1 tablespoon butter

4 tablespoons minced fresh parsley

salt and freshly ground pepper to taste

Put the potatoes into a pot with a steaming trivet or rack. Bring the water to a rapid boil. Reduce heat and continue steaming until the potatoes are easily pierced with a sharp knife, or about 12 minutes. If the potatoes finish cooking before you are ready to serve, remove the pot from heat and cock the lid slightly. Toss the potatoes with butter, minced parsley, salt and pepper just before serving.

Pan Poached Fish

¾ lb. fresh fish (steaks or fillets) or 1 small dressed fish

1 tablespoon butter

3 green onions or 2 shallots, minced

1 clove garlic, pressed

½ cup chicken stock or dry white wine

salt and pepper to taste

1 lemon, cut into wedges (optional garnish)

Set a platter in the oven to warm. Rinse the fish in cold water and pat dry. In a large heavy skillet, melt 1 tablespoon butter. Sauté the green onion or shallots over medium heat until limp. Stir in the garlic. Add the stock or wine. Bring to a boil; reduce heat to medium low. Lay the fish in the pan and cover. Simmer just until the fish turns opaque and flakes, or about 10 minutes per inch thickness of fish. (Allow twice as long for frozen fish.) When the fish is done, move it to the warm platter with a slotted spatula. Over high heat, quickly reduce the cooking liquid; season with salt and pepper to taste and ladle over the fish. Garnish with lemon wedges, if desired.

Some of the first chipped stone tools that mark the beginning of human culture were used to spear fish. By the Iron Age (about 1000 B. C. in southern Europe), people were fishing with barbed hooks, using nets with heavy sinkers and line-fishing from boats offshore. They were catching pike, bream, perch, dogfish, cod, flounder, eel, haddock, mackerel and whiting, just to name some of the more familiar species. The fishing industry began in the Middle Ages with the advent of commercial herring fishing.

Hearty Tuna Chowder
Watercress-Dressed Zucchini
Garlic French Bread or Pita

SERVES 4

TIME TO PREPARE

20 minutes

INGREDIENTS

ON HAND
- ☐ *flour*
- ☐ *milk (3 cups)*
- ☐ *butter*
- ☐ *olive oil*
- ☐ *white wine vinegar*
- ☐ *Dijon-type mustard*
- ☐ *fresh or powdered garlic*
- ☐ *thyme*
- ☐ *dill weed*
- ☐ *dried tarragon*
- ☐ *paprika*

SHOPPING LIST
- ☐ *2 6 ½-oz. cans of waterpacked tuna*
- ☐ *4 oz. Farmer's, Jack or medium cheddar cheese*
- ☐ *pita or French bread*
- ☐ *celery*
- ☐ *fresh parsley*
- ☐ *4 green onions or 1 medium yellow onion*
- ☐ *1 medium potato*
- ☐ *4 small zucchini*
- ☐ *1 bunch watercress (or rocket, also called roquette, rugula or arugula)*
- ☐ *1 lemon*

Tuna are truly magnificent fish, and have qualities impossible to recognize upon opening the convenient can. For instance, they are the second swiftest fish in the ocean (sailfish are the only faster swimmers), and can travel at a rate of 20 times their length per second, or close to 50 m.p.h.

The worldwide consumption of tuna has nearly doubled in the past 15 years to 1.5 million tons per year. The modern fisherman can hunt tuna with infrared rays, airplanes, helicopters, and even satellites. Tuna ships use nets that cover 25 acres and are dropped to a depth of 6500 feet. As much as a ton of tuna can be taken in one haul.

OVERVIEW

1. Prepare the garlic bread and place in oven.

2. Prepare the tuna chowder.

3. While the chowder is cooking, prepare the salad.

Garlic French or Pita Bread

FRENCH BREAD:

Cut the bread lengthwise. Butter and sprinkle with garlic powder, fresh or dried parsley and paprika. Slice the bread into pieces but don't cut all the way through. Put the two halves back together, wrap in foil and warm in a 350° oven. For a crusty top, put the buttered side of the bread under the broiler for a minute right before serving. True garlic afficionados can press garlic cloves right on the buttered bread and spread.

PITA BREAD:

Cut horizontally like an English muffin. Brush with butter and sprinkle with garlic, parsley and paprika. Place on a cookie sheet in a 325° oven for 5 to 7 minutes.

Hearty Tuna Chowder

2 tablespoons butter

½ cup chopped celery

1 medium yellow onion, chopped
or 4 green onions, sliced

1 medium potato, peeled and
chopped into tiny pieces

3 tablespoons flour

3 cups milk

2 6½ oz. cans waterpacked tuna

4 oz. Farmer's, Jack or cheddar
cheese, grated

½ teaspoon thyme

½ teaspoon dill weed

salt and freshly ground pepper
to taste

¼ cup chopped parsley

In a heavy soup pot, melt the butter and sauté the celery, onion and potato for 5 minutes, or until the potato is soft. Sprinkle in the flour and mix thoroughly. Add the milk slowly, stirring constantly. Continue to stir until the mixture thickens. Stir in the tuna, cheese, thyme and dill. Season with salt and freshly ground pepper to taste. Heat over medium low heat until thoroughly warmed, but do not bring to a boil. Garnish each serving with chopped fresh parsley.

This chowder could be enhanced with additional vegetables. Chop them into small pieces and sauté with the onions.

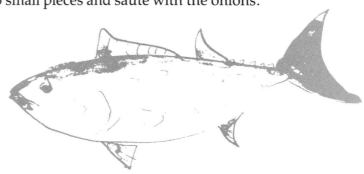

Watercress-Dressed Zucchini

2 tablespoons olive oil

2 teaspoons fresh lemon juice

1 teaspoon white wine vinegar

½ teaspoon Dijon-type mustard

a pinch of dried tarragon

4 small zucchini, thinly sliced

¼ cup minced watercress leaves
(or rocket—also called roquette,
rugula or arugula)

salt and fresh ground pepper
to taste

Whisk together the oil, lemon juice, vinegar, mustard, tarragon, salt and pepper in a bowl suitable for holding the entire salad. Add the zucchini and watercress. Toss.

Fillets Florentine

Rice

SERVES 2

TIME TO PREPARE

30 minutes

INGREDIENTS

ON HAND

- ☐ *brown rice*
- ☐ *flour*
- ☐ *1 egg*
- ☐ *milk (½ cup)*
- ☐ *Parmesan cheese (¼ cup)*
- ☐ *butter*
- ☐ *vegetable oil*
- ☐ *dry sherry*
- ☐ *¼ cup toasted slivered almonds (optional)*

SHOPPING LIST

- ☐ *½ to ¾ lb. fish fillets (sole, turbot, halibut, flounder, rock fish, or cod will do)*
- ☐ *1 10-oz. package frozen chopped spinach*
- ☐ *½ lb. fresh mushrooms*

This is a simplified, low-fat version of the classic recipe. The richness of the sauce is provided by an abundance of mushrooms sautéed in sherry rather than the traditional heavy cream and butter.

OVERVIEW

1. If you precooked rice in the morning, complete cooking the rice now. With precooked rice (*see page 99 for directions*) this meal will take 30 minutes to cook. If you are starting rice from scratch it will take 45 to 50 minutes.

2. Prepare the sauce.

3. Begin cooking the spinach.

4. Start to cook the fish, which will take about 8 to 30 minutes to prepare. (See time table for cooking fish.)

5. When the fish is nearly cooked, gently reheat the sauce.

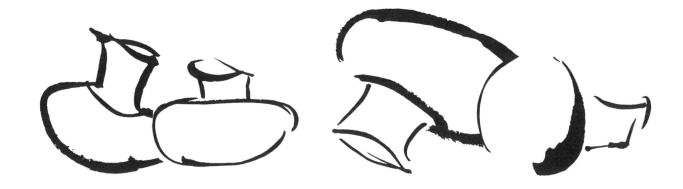

Fillets Florentine

SAUCE

½ lb. fresh mushrooms, sliced

¼ teaspoon salt

1 tablespoon sherry

1 tablespoon butter

1 tablespoon flour

½ cup milk

1 egg yolk slightly beaten with 2 tablespoons milk

¼ cup freshly grated Parmesan cheese

1 10-oz. package frozen chopped spinach

½ to ¾ lb. fillets (sole, turbot, halibut, flounder, rock fish or cod will do)

vegetable oil

toasted slivered almonds (optional garnish)

Warm a skillet over medium heat. Quickly stir in the sliced mushrooms, salt and sherry and cover the pan. Cook for 5 minutes or until the mushrooms are tender. Stir once or twice, but be careful not to let the liquid steam away. When the mushrooms are cooked, reduce the liquid to 1 tablespoon and transfer to a bowl.

Rinse and dry the skillet and make the sauce: Melt 1 tablespoon butter in the skillet and brown the flour in it, stirring constantly. Add in ½ cup milk in small amounts, making sure the sauce is stirred smooth before adding more milk. Next stir in the egg yolk and milk mixture, and then the Parmesan cheese. Continue stirring just until the Parmesan melts. Stir in the mushrooms, remove from heat and set aside.

Begin cooking the frozen spinach over medium low heat. Rinse the fillets in cold water and pat dry with paper towels. Fry the fish in a lightly oiled pan. If the fillets are less than ½ inch thick, they do not need to be turned.

TIME TABLE FOR COOKING FRESH FISH

½ inch or less	2 to 4 minutes
½ to ¾ inch	4 to 8 minutes
1 to 1 ½ inches	10 to 15 minutes

Frozen fish will take approximately twice as long to cook. Do not thaw fish before cooking.

As the fish cooks, gently reheat the sauce. Do not bring it to a boil! Lay the fish atop a nest of spinach. Generously sauce and sprinkle with slivered almonds, if desired. Serve immediately.

Steamed Fish Wrapped in Seaweed

Orange and Ginger Dipping Sauce

Broccoli Salad

Rice

SERVES 2

(easily doubled)

TIME TO PREPARE

30 minutes

INGREDIENTS

ON HAND

☐ *brown or converted rice*
☐ *olive oil*
☐ *Chinese sesame oil*
☐ *rice vinegar*
☐ *soy sauce*
☐ *capers*
☐ *fresh ginger*

SHOPPING LIST

☐ *½ to ¾ lb. fish fillets (snapper, halibut, grouper, rockfish or bass)*
☐ *1 bunch broccoli*
☐ *nori seaweed*
☐ *wasabi (powdered Japanese horseradish, optional)*
☐ *1 orange*
☐ *1 lemon*

Nori seaweed, which comes in flat square sheets, and *wasabi*, a green powdered form of horseradish, are available at Asian markets as well as many supermarkets. If you presoak the brown rice (*see Techniques of Quick Cooking, p.99*), or use converted rice, this meal will take only 30 minutes to prepare. If you are starting rice from scratch allow 15 or 20 minutes more.

OVERVIEW

1. Start cooking rice.

2. Prepare the Broccoli Salad.

3. Prepare the dipping sauce.

4. Prepare the steamed fish. (Use the pot in which you cooked the broccoli to reduce clean-up.)

Orange and Ginger Dipping Sauce

Combine all the ingredients and let sit to blend flavors.

1 tablespoon soy sauce	¼ teaspoon grated orange peel
1 tablespoon rice vinegar	2 tablespoons fresh orange juice
¼ teaspoon grated ginger root	½ teaspoon Chinese sesame oil

Broccoli Salad

1 bunch fresh broccoli

2 tablespoons olive oil

3 teaspoons lemon juice

1 tablespoon rinsed and chopped capers

salt and freshly ground pepper to taste

Bring a pot of water to a boil. Cut off the flowerets of the broccoli; reserve the stalks for another use. Break up the flowerets into similar sized pieces. Prepare a bowl with ice and water. Plunge the broccoli into the boiling water and cook for 30 seconds. Drain in colander, then immediately transfer the broccoli to ice water. When the broccoli has cooled, drain again, then wrap in paper towels to absorb the excess moisture. Combine the remaining ingredients in a bowl; stir in the broccoli. Season with freshly ground pepper and salt to taste. Set aside.

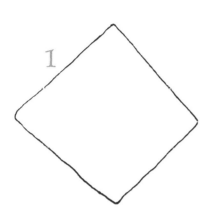

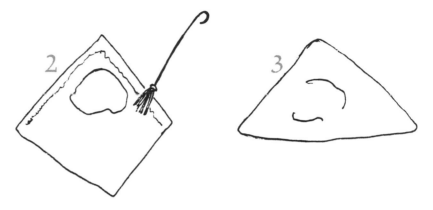

Steamed Fish Wrapped in Seaweed

½ to ¾ lb. fish fillets (snapper, rockfish, bass, grouper or halibut)

2 or 4 sheets nori seaweed

1 tablespoon wasabi (powdered Japanese horseradish, optional)

If you are especially fond of nori, divide the fish into 4 equal portions. Otherwise, divide it into 2 portions. If you are using wasabi, mix 1 tablespoon with 2 to 3 tablespoons of water to make a thick paste.

Angle a sheet of nori in front of you so that it is diamond-shaped. Place a portion of fish in the center of the upper triangle. You want the fish to be 1 inch thick, so fold the undulating outline of the fillet back upon itself, if necessary. Brush the fish with wasabi, if desired.

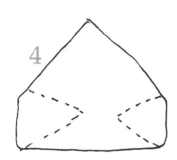

Moisten the upper edge of the diamond with water (a pastry brush is handy) then fold the lower half of the nori across the fish and press along the edge. Now roll the package away from you so that you catch the tip under the weight of the fish. Tuck under the two wings so that you have a neat package. Repeat this operation with each portion of fish.

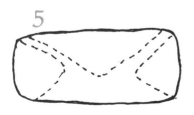

Set the fish on an Oriental steaming rack. Or, put a dish on a regular steaming trivet set in a pot with water. Lay the rolls of stuffed seaweed on the dish so that they don't touch one another, and place a towel under the pot's lid to absorb the condensation. Steam gently for 8 minutes per 1 inch thickness of fish. Do not overcook. Serve immediately with the rice and salad and small bowls of dipping sauce.

Fish Chowder

Tossed Greens with Vinaigrette Dressing

Warm Crusty Bread

SERVES 6

TIME TO PREPARE

50 minutes

INGREDIENTS

ON HAND

☐ *vegetable oil*
☐ *olive oil*
☐ *red or white wine vinegar*
☐ *Dijon-type mustard*
☐ *dry white wine*
☐ *anisette*
☐ *fresh garlic*
☐ *1 whole dried hot red pepper*
☐ *dried or fresh thyme*
☐ *bay leaf*
☐ *saffron (optional)*
☐ *fish broth (3 cups, optional) or clam juice (1 ½ cup, optional)*

SHOPPING LIST

☐ *1 ¾ lbs. fish fillets suitable for chowder (for example, rock fish or snapper)*
☐ *1 28-oz. can whole peeled tomatoes*
☐ *2 yellow onions*
☐ *1 bunch leeks or 2 bunches green onions*
☐ *3 red bell peppers*
☐ *salad greens for 6*
☐ *3 medium-sized red potatoes*
☐ *1 bunch fresh parsley*
☐ *½ pint heavy cream*
☐ *1 loaf good crusty bread*

A modest amount of heavy cream, hot red pepper and anisette gives this chowder a simple, delicious elegance. It is a variation of a chowder created by Pierre Franey and is the best fish chowder I have ever tasted—a sentiment echoed by the many guests to whom it's been served.

OVERVIEW

1. Prepare the salad dressing and greens. (*See page 100 for Vinaigrette Dressings.*) Cover and chill the salad greens until ready to toss with dressing and serve.

2. Wrap the bread in foil and warm in a slow oven.

3. Prepare the Fish Chowder.

Recent research has come to the surprising conclusion that the oil in fatty fish actually lowers the blood's cholesterol level. This helps to explain why Eskimos generally have low blood cholesterol levels although they eat a diet relatively high in fat. The research concludes that certain oily fish, including Atlantic mackerel, herring, sardines, rainbow trout, salmon, Pacific oysters, squid, striped mullet, blue fin tuna and albacore have a definite salutary effect on our blood's cholesterol level. Delightful news.

Fish Chowder

1 ¾ lbs. fish fillets (rock fish or snapper)

2 tablespoons olive oil

1 cup chopped yellow onion

2 cloves garlic, minced

2 cups coarsely diced red bell pepper (use green if red bells are not available)

1 ½ cups thinly sliced leeks or green onions, including the tender green portion of the stem

1 teaspoon powdered saffron (optional)

1 whole dried hot red pepper

½ teaspoon salt or more to taste

¼ teaspoon freshly ground black pepper

½ teaspoon dried thyme or 2 sprigs fresh thyme

1 bay leaf

1 28-oz. can whole tomatoes, drained and chopped (reserve liquid)

1 cup dry white wine

1 cup potatoes cut into ½-inch cubes

3 cups liquid (fish stock, or reserved juice from tomatoes plus water and/or up to 1 ½ cups clam juice)

½ cup heavy cream

2 tablespoons anisette

¼ cup minced fresh parsley

Remove any bones from the fish; cut into bite-sized pieces. Heat the oil in a large pot. Sauté the yellow onion until it wilts, then stir in the garlic, bell pepper, leeks or green onions and saffron. Stir for 1 minute, adding some wine if the pot gets dry.

Stir in the whole red pepper, salt, pepper, thyme and bay leaf. Cover; cook 3 to 5 minutes. Chop the canned tomatoes and add them to the pot. Stir for 1 minute. Add the wine and cubed potatoes. Cover and simmer 10 minutes.

Add the fish stock or water. Stir. Test the potatoes. If they are soft, add the fish. Simmer 5 minutes.

Stir in the cream and warm thoroughly, but do not boil. Add the anisette, stir gently and remove the hot pepper and bay leaf. Adjust seasonings. Ladle the soup into warm bowls. Sprinkle with minced fresh parsley.

Tossed Greens with Vinaigrette Dressing

See page 100 for instructions.

Crispy Baked Fish

Yogurt Dill Sauce

New Potatoes with Pesto

Sautéed Zucchini with Garlic and Lemon

SERVES 3 TO 4

TIME TO PREPARE

30 to 40 minutes

INGREDIENTS

ON HAND

☐ *pesto (or see page 107 for recipes)*
☐ *2 slices dried out bread*
☐ *1 egg*
☐ *Parmesan cheese (¼ cup)*
☐ *butter*
☐ *vegetable oil*
☐ *olive oil*
☐ *Dijon-type mustard*
☐ *leaf thyme*
☐ *paprika*
☐ *fresh or dried dill weed*

SHOPPING LIST

☐ *1 ½ lbs. fish fillets, ¾ to 1 inch thick*
☐ *12 golf ball-sized new potatoes (about 1 ¼ lbs.)*
☐ *1 bunch green onions*
☐ *3 or 4 zucchini*
☐ *1 lemon*
☐ *8 oz. plain low-fat yogurt*

This method of cooking fish gives you a crispy coating like battered fried fish—without the butter or oil. The herbs and Parmesan cheese impart such a nice flavor that you won't miss the oiliness of the fried version. The Yogurt-Dill Sauce is a fresh, piquant alternative to tartar sauce.

OVERVIEW

1. Preheat the oven to 500°. Prepare the baking pan and place it in the oven.

2. Scrub the potatoes. Begin to steam them.

3. Prepare the pesto if you haven't any on hand. (*See page 107 for recipes.*)

4. Prepare the crumb mixture for the fish. Lightly beat an egg in a bowl suitable for dipping the fish.

5. Prepare the Yogurt-Dill Sauce.

6. Coat the fish with the egg and crumb mixture. Place in the preheated baking pan and begin baking the fish.

7. Sauté the zucchini. Drain the potatoes and toss with pesto.

Yogurt-Dill Sauce

Stir together the ingredients.

1 cup plain low-fat yogurt

½ teaspoon minced fresh dill weed or ¼ teaspoon dried dill weed

¼ teaspoon Dijon-type mustard

½ cup finely sliced green onions (include crisp green stem)

New Potatoes with Pesto

12 small new potatoes (about
      1 ¼ lbs.)

2 to 4 tablespoons pesto (see
      page 107 for recipes)

salt and freshly ground pepper to
      taste

Scrub clean the potatoes and place them on a steaming trivet set over water in a covered pot. Bring the water to a boil. Reduce the heat and steam until the potatoes are easily pierced with the tip of a knife, or about 20 minutes. Drain the water and remove the trivet from the pot. Toss the potatoes with pesto. Start with 2 tablespoons and add more if you wish. Season with salt and freshly ground pepper. If the potatoes finish cooking before you are ready to serve, remove the pot from the heat and cock the lid slightly to allow some steam to escape. The potatoes will stay warm.

Crispy Baked Fish

1 ½ lb. fresh fish fillets, ¾ to 1
      inch thick

1 egg (If you are concerned about
      cholesterol, use the egg white
      only.)

CRUMB COATING

½ cup fine dry bread crumbs

¼ cup freshly grated Parmesan
      cheese

¼ teaspoon leaf thyme

¼ teaspoon paprika

Whirl bits of dried out bread in a food processor or blender until you get ½ cup crumbs of fine consistency. Add remaining ingredients and blend together. You could make a larger quantity of the crumb mixture to keep on hand in the freezer.

Rub a baking pan with oil and set it in a 500° oven. Rinse and pat dry the fish; cut into serving-size pieces. Dip the fish into the egg and then the crumbs, patting the fish with as much as will adhere. Place the pieces of fish at least 1 inch apart on the hot pan and return to the oven.

A 1-inch thick fillet will take approximately 10 minutes to cook. (*See table on page 37.*) *Do not overcook the fish.* You are not using butter or oil, but relying on the natural juices of the fish for its moistness. The fish is done when the thickest part of the fillet is barely opaque and still moist when prodded.

Sautéed Zucchini with Garlic and Lemon

3 or 4 zucchini

½ teaspoon olive oil

½ teaspoon butter

fresh lemon juice to taste (start
      with ½ teaspoon)

garlic powder (optional)

salt and freshly ground pepper to
      taste

Thinly slice the zucchini. Heat the oil and butter. Sauté the zucchini over medium high heat until just barely tender, which will take only about 2 minutes. Cover the skillet between stirrings. If the pan seems dry, add 1 tablespoon water. Sprinkle with lemon juice, a dash of garlic powder if desired, and salt and pepper to taste. Serve immediately.

Grilled Fish Brushed with Hot Sesame Oil

Buckwheat Noodles with Braised Green Onions

Mung Bean Sprouts and Cherry Tomato Salad

SERVES 2

TIME TO PREPARE

20 minutes

INGREDIENTS

ON HAND
- [ ] *vegetable oil*
- [ ] *Chinese sesame oil*
- [ ] *soy sauce*
- [ ] *Tabasco*
- [ ] *fresh garlic*
- [ ] *anise*
- [ ] *fresh mint (optional)*

SHOPPING LIST
- [ ] *¾ lb. fillets of firm white fish (halibut, rock fish, shark, etc.)*
- [ ] *6 oz. buckwheat noodles*
- [ ] *1 bunch green onions*
- [ ] *2 cups mung bean sprouts*
- [ ] *1 lemon*
- [ ] *10 cherry tomatoes*
- [ ] *1 red bell pepper (optional)*

OVERVIEW

1. Prepare the salad and dressing.

2. Start to boil a large pot of water for the noodles. Turn on the broiler if you've an electric stove.

3. Prepare fish for broiling; prepare basting sauce. Begin boiling noodles.

4. Begin to broil the fish.

5. When the noodles are *al dente*, pour them into a colander. Rinse under very warm water and drain well. Using the same pot, braise the green onions.

6. Finish preparing the noodles.

Mung Bean Sprouts and Cherry Tomato Salad

2 cups mung bean sprouts, rinsed in cold water

10 cherry tomatoes, stemmed and halved

3 tablespoons minced red bell pepper (optional)

DRESSING

1 tablespoon light vegetable oil

1 tablespoon fresh lemon juice

¼ teaspoon anise

4 to 6 fresh mint leaves, minced (optional)

On the bottom of a salad bowl, combine ingredients for the dressing. Put remaining ingredients into the bowl; toss just before serving.

Grilled Fish Brushed with Hot Sesame Oil

¾ lb. fillets of firm white fish (halibut, rock fish, etc.—shark is also good prepared this way)

BASTING SAUCE

3 tablespoons soy sauce

1 tablespoon Chinese sesame oil

½ teaspoon Tabasco

Rub a baking pan with a little vegetable oil. Rinse fish and pat dry; lay in pan. Liberally brush with basting sauce. Broil 4 inches below the heating element. A 1-inch thick fillet will take 10 minutes total cooking time. (A frozen fillet will take twice as long to cook and should be placed further from the heating element so that the surface doesn't dry out before the interior is cooked.) When the fish is flakey and cooked halfway through, flip gently with a spatula and brush liberally with basting sauce. Fillets less than ½ inch thick need not be turned. Fish is done when the fish flakes all the way through and the flesh is opaque. Do not overcook. (See table on page 37).

Buckwheat Noodles with Braised Green Onions

6 oz. buckwheat noodles

1 teaspoon Chinese sesame oil

1 bunch green onions

Bring a pot of salted water to a boil. Cook the noodles until *al dente*, or about 7 minutes. Drain the noodles in a colander; rinse under very warm running water. Shake colander to remove excess water.

Heat the sesame oil over medium high heat. Rinse and trim the green onions, leaving short green tails. Slice the onions lengthwise into strips and then into 2-inch lengths. Stir into the hot oil and sauté for 5 seconds. Remove the green onions from the pot. Return noodles to the pot; toss with 1 to 2 tablespoons of basting sauce. Make a bed of noodles on warm plates. Lay the fish atop the noodles; pour remaining juices in the baking dish over the fish. Garnish with braised green onions.

Pan-Fried Trout with Anchovy Paste and Sherry

Couscous with Pine Nuts

Sautéed Red Cabbage

SERVES 2

TIME TO PREPARE

20 minutes

INGREDIENTS

ON HAND
- ☐ *flour*
- ☐ *butter*
- ☐ *dry white wine*
- ☐ *dry sherry*
- ☐ *anchovy paste*

SHOPPING LIST
- ☐ *2 small or 1 large trout*
- ☐ *¾ cup couscous*
- ☐ *1 small head red cabbage*
- ☐ *1 oz. pine nuts*
- ☐ *1 lemon*

This may be the fastest elegant meal possible. The red cabbage is a nutritive painterly touch that complements the rest of the meal's textures and flavors.

Couscous, the staple of northern Africa, can be made from millet, rice or wheat flour, but you will most commonly encounter wheat couscous in the US. It can be purchased in bulk at health food stores or packaged in supermarkets and grocery stores specializing in Middle Eastern foodstuffs.

There is some debate regarding the derivation of the word "couscous." Leon Isnard, who wrote a book on African cooking, concluded that the name is simply onomatopoeic, imitative of the sound of steam passing through the holes of the traditional cooking utensil. The preparation of your couscous, placed in a simple pot and cooked by pouring boiling water over it, will be much faster than the traditional cooking method, but unfortunately silent.

OVERVIEW

1. Lightly toast the pine nuts. Rinse and cut the cabbage.

2. Rinse and pat dry the fish. Dredge in flour. Begin to boil water for couscous.

3. Begin to fry the trout. As soon as you turn the trout, pour boiling water over the couscous and start to sauté the cabbage.

Pan-Fried Trout with Anchovy Paste and Sherry

2 small or 1 large trout

flour

1 tablespoon butter

¼ teaspoon anchovy paste

2 tablespoons dry sherry

1 lemon, cut into wedges

The fish should be scaled and gutted, but ideally have the head and tail still attached; the flesh will stay moister during cooking. Rinse the fish in cold water and pat dry with paper towels. Dredge lightly in flour. In a large heavy skillet, melt the butter over medium heat and stir in the anchovy paste. Lay the fish in the skillet. Fry for exactly 6 minutes on each side. During its last minute of cooking, splash with sherry. Garnish with lemon before serving.

Couscous with Pine Nuts

¾ cup couscous

¾ cup boiling water

4 teaspoons pine nuts

salt to taste

Over medium low heat, lightly toast the pine nuts in heavy skillet. Stir continuously for they burn very quickly. Set toasted nuts aside.

Bring the water to a boil. Stir in the couscous, pine nuts and salt. Immediately cover and remove from heat. Let sit for 5 minutes. Fluff gently with a fork or chopsticks just before serving.

Sautéed Red Cabbage

½ small dense red cabbage

2 tablespoons dry white wine or dry sherry or sauterne

1 teaspoon light vegetable oil

salt to taste

Rinse cabbage; remove old outer leaves and core. Coarsely cut into pieces. Heat the oil in a large pot with a tight-fitting lid. Stir in the cabbage and wine; sprinkle lightly with salt. Cover pot; cook over medium heat for 3 to 5 minutes, stirring quickly once or twice while checking its progress. When tender-crisp, serve immediately with the trout and couscous.

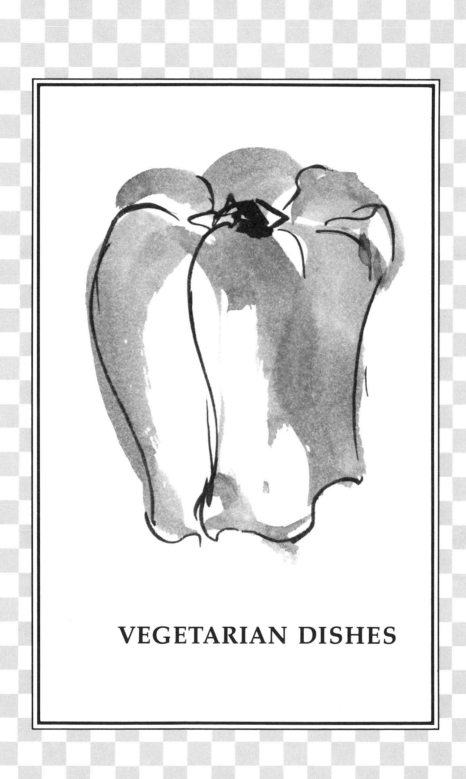

VEGETARIAN DISHES

Mexican Millet

Warmed Tortillas or Crusty Bread

Tossed Greens with Vinaigrette

SERVES 2

(easily doubled)

TIME TO PREPARE

15 to 50 minutes

INGREDIENTS

ON HAND

- ☐ ½ *cup raw or 1 cup cooked grain (millet, bulgur or brown rice)*
- ☐ *vegetable oil*
- ☐ *olive oil*
- ☐ *wine vinegar*
- ☐ *fresh garlic*
- ☐ *chili powder*
- ☐ *oregano*

SHOPPING LIST

- ☐ *1 15-oz. can kidney beans or 2 cups homecooked*
- ☐ *1 8-oz. can tomato sauce*
- ☐ *4 oz. ricotta or cottage cheese*
- ☐ *2 oz. cheddar cheese*
- ☐ *1 package of corn tortillas or 1 loaf of crusty bread*
- ☐ *2 zucchini*
- ☐ *1 bell pepper*
- ☐ *salad greens for 2*
- ☐ *4 oz. tofu (optional)*
- ☐ *Optional garnishes for Mexican Millet:*
  black olives
  green onions
  cornchips

This stove-top casserole is open to many variations. Bulgur or rice could be substituted for millet. If you have cooked grain on hand, this meal will take only 15 minutes to prepare.

Millet takes 45 minutes to cook—3 parts water to 1 part millet—and has a tendency to get mushy. The best way to achieve fluffy millet is to boil the millet in its cooking water for 7 minutes in the morning, turn off the heat and let it sit all day in the covered pot. The millet will be perfectly cooked in the evening. If you bring the millet to a boil in the morning and immediately turn off the heat, the grain will take only 10 to 15 minutes to cook in the evening. Either shortcut will considerably reduce meal preparation time in the evening.

Millet is a member of the plant family *Graminae*, better known to us as grass. All of the grains we eat are the seeds of grasses (except for buckwheat and amaranth); in fact, 80% of the world's agriculture is devoted to growing grasses.

OVERVIEW

1. Begin cooking the grain unless you have 1 cup cooked grain on hand.

2. Prepare the salad dressing and greens. (*See page 100 for Vinaigrette Dressings.*) Cover and chill the salad greens until ready to toss with dressing and serve.

3. About 15 minutes before the grain is finished cooking, begin to warm the tortillas. Start the recipe for Mexican Millet.

Warm Tortillas

Turn on oven to 325°. Lay a clean dish towel that has been lightly sprinkled with water on a cookie sheet. Place tortillas on the towel so that they are not overlapping. Cover the tortillas with another clean dish towel and lightly sprinkle the second towel with water. Place in the oven for 10 to 15 minutes.

Mexican Millet

2   tablespoons olive oil

1   tablespoon chili powder

3   large cloves garlic, pressed

2   zucchini, sliced

1   bell pepper, coarsely chopped

1   cup cooked millet, bulgur or brown rice

4   oz. tofu, crumbled (optional)

2   cups cooked kidney beans, or 1 15-oz. can, drained and rinsed

½   cup tomato sauce

a pinch of oregano

½   cup ricotta or cottage cheese

½   cup grated cheddar cheese

OPTIONAL GARNISHES

½   cup chopped green onion; a handful of crumbled cornchips; sliced pitted black olives

Heat the oil in a large frying pan over medium heat. Stir in the chili powder and pressed garlic. Add the zucchini and bell pepper. Sauté the vegetables until they are tender-crisp; then stir in the cooked millet, optional tofu and kidney beans. Stir the tomato sauce and oregano into the ricotta or cottage cheese; pour this mixture into the frying pan. Stir, top with grated cheese and cover. Cook over low heat until the cheese is melted. Garnish and serve with the warm tortillas and tossed salad.

The fields of wild grasses that sprang up towards the end of the Ice Age drew together the first villages of humans. An archaeologist named J. R. Harlan once tried to discover what sort of harvest a prehistoric family could achieve from intensive efforts. He entered a field of densely growing wild grain with a flint-bladed sickle in hand and in one hour, reaped enough to provide over two pounds of clean grain. Harlan figured that in only three weeks of harvesting, a family of six could provide themselves with a year's supply of one pound of grain per person per day. What's more, the wild grain provided twice as much protein as our domesticated variety.

Tossed Greens with Vinaigrette Dressing

See page 100 for instructions.

Spinach Ricotta Pie

Cherry Tomato Salad

Herbed-Parmesan-Garlic French Bread

SERVES 3 TO 4

TIME TO PREPARE

45 minutes

INGREDIENTS

ON HAND

☐ *flour*
☐ *3 eggs*
☐ *butter (¼ lb.)*
☐ *olive oil*
☐ *red wine vinegar*
☐ *Dijon-type mustard*
☐ *fresh garlic*
☐ *fresh mint (optional)*
☐ *fresh or dried dill weed*
☐ *garlic salt (optional)*
☐ *2 hard-boiled eggs (optional)*

SHOPPING LIST

☐ *1 pint part-skim ricotta cheese*
☐ *2 to 4 oz. cheese (feta is good, but any cheese will do)*
☐ *2 oz. Parmesan cheese*
☐ *1 10-oz. package frozen chopped spinach*
☐ *4 large green onions*
☐ *fresh parsley*
☐ *fresh chives*
☐ *1 lemon*
☐ *1 ¼ lbs. cherry tomatoes*
☐ *1 loaf French bread*
☐ *1 Italian sausage (optional)*

Fresh spinach is a labor intensive vegetable to prepare, so let me extol the virtues of frozen spinach. Here is a vegetable that suffers little in being frozen. Properly prepared frozen spinach tastes almost exactly like cooked fresh spinach. And according to the USDA's *Nutritive Value of American Foods* (Agriculture Handbook #456), frozen spinach is superior in nutritive value to the "fresh" spinach you buy at your supermarket.

	Calcium (mg.)	Iron (mg.)	Vitamin A (mg.)	Vitamin C (mg.)
Fresh spinach leaves, cooked	167	4.0	14,580	50
Frozen chopped spinach, cooked	249	4.6	17,380	42

You could substitute cottage cheese in the Spinach Pie recipe but nutritionally speaking, ricotta cheese is superior to cottage cheese because much of the calcium in cottage cheese separates out with the whey. A cup of cottage cheese contains only 138 milligrams calcium compared to approximately 400 milligrams in a cup of ricotta.

OVERVIEW

1. Prepare the Spinach Ricotta Pie. Put in oven to bake.

2. Prepare the Cherry Tomato Salad. Chill.

3. Prepare the Herbed-Parmesan-Garlic French Bread. Wrap in foil and place in oven.

Spinach Ricotta Pie

1 10-oz. package frozen chopped
  spinach

1 pint (2 cups) ricotta cheese

3 eggs, lightly beaten

3 tablespoons whole wheat flour

3 large green onions, thinly sliced
  (include fresh green stem)

2 teaspoons minced fresh dill
  weed, or 1 teaspoon dried dill
  weed

2 to 4 oz. diced cheese (crumbled
  feta is very good)

1 Italian sausage (optional)

1 tablespoon chopped fresh mint
  (optional)

Preheat the oven to 350°. If you are going to use sausage, poke it all over with a fork and poach it in a small amount of boiling water for 5 to 10 minutes. This will reduce its fat content. Under gently running cold water, peel away the casing. Chop the meat.

As the sausage poaches, thaw the spinach by placing it on a steaming trivet over boiling water. You want to be able to just fork the spinach apart, not cook it. When the spinach is ready, drain the water and remove the trivet. Return the spinach to the pot and stir in the remaining ingredients plus the optional sausage.

Pour into a lightly oiled 9-inch round pie pan. Bake for 30 minutes or until firm. Remove from oven and let the pie sit for a few minutes before serving.

Cherry Tomato Salad

1 ¼ lbs. ripe cherry
    tomatoes (4 generous cups)

2 hard-boiled eggs (optional)

DRESSING

2 tablespoons olive oil

½ teaspoon Dijon-type mustard

1 tablespoon red wine vinegar

Combine the dressing ingredients. Stem and halve the tomatoes; stir in the dressing. Salt and pepper to taste. Chill until serving. Garnish with grated hard-boiled eggs and more fresh dill, if desired.

2 teaspoons minced fresh dill
  weed or 1 teaspoon dried dill
  weed

2 teaspoons fresh lemon juice

1 tablespoon chopped fresh
  parsley

1 green onion, thinly sliced

Herbed-Parmesan-Garlic French Bread

3 cloves garlic

4 tablespoons chopped chives

2 tablespoons chopped fresh
  parsley

2 tablespoons olive oil

¼ lb. butter (1 stick)

½ cup freshly grated Parmesan
  cheese

garlic salt (optional)

Blend together the ingredients either by softening the butter first or by using a blender or processor. Slice the French bread horizontally and spread. Lightly sprinkle with garlic salt. If you want a crisp top crust, after removing the spinach pie, unwrap the bread and let the top crisp under the broiler for a moment.

To freeze the extra spread: shape in a cylinder and wrap well. Cut off as much as you want at a time. This spread is wonderful in soups, brushed on broiled fish or chicken, with steamed or baked potatoes, noodles, and steamed vegetables. It is so highly flavored that a little bit of butter goes a long way.

Eggplant Szechuan with Buckwheat Noodles

Mung Bean, Green Onion and Sesame Seed Salad

SERVES 2

TIME TO PREPARE

30 minutes

INGREDIENTS

ON HAND
- [ ] *chicken stock (½ cup)*
- [ ] *fresh lemon juice or rice vinegar*
- [ ] *vegetable oil*
- [ ] *Chinese sesame oil*
- [ ] *soy sauce*
- [ ] *sugar*
- [ ] *fresh garlic*
- [ ] *fresh ginger*
- [ ] *sesame seeds*
- [ ] *anise seeds (optional)*
- [ ] *rice (optional)*

SHOPPING LIST
- [ ] *1 medium-sized eggplant*
- [ ] *5 green onions*
- [ ] *2 cups mung bean sprouts*
- [ ] *fresh cilantro or parsley*
- [ ] *fresh chives*
- [ ] *buckwheat noodles (8 oz.) or other noodles*
- [ ] *Chinese black bean paste*
- [ ] *Chinese dark vinegar*
- [ ] *dried red pepper flakes*

Eggplant Szechuan is rather spicy as are many dishes that originate from that part of China (*see page 10*). The recipe calls for Chinese black bean paste, dark vinegar and dried red pepper flakes, all of which can be found in Asian markets or gourmet shops, or in your local supermarket. Other types of noodles or rice can be substituted for buckwheat noodles.

Stir-frying is really the ideal way of quick cooking. Once you catch on to the basic ways to sauce a stir-fried dish, you'll see that you can prepare a fast meal for any number of people or just yourself with whatever fresh vegetables and bits of meat, fish or tofu you have on hand.

This method of quick cuisine was developed by the agricultural workers of China who lived from spring until harvest in small, isolated huts out in the fields. Fuel for cooking posed a real problem. The brush growing on nearby land was either too green to burn or soon gone, there were few or no draft animals to provide dried dung, and wood or charcoal had to be transported, so it was necessary that cooking use an absolute minimum of fuel. Vegetables and meat were cut into sliver-like pieces which would cook quickly over a fast, hot fire. The wok adds to the efficiency of stir-frying; its bowl-like shape concentrates heat in a small area which makes possible the high temperature sautéing-steaming. Stir-frying!

OVERVIEW

1. Prepare Mung Bean Salad and dressing. Cover and chill.

2. Sauté the eggplant. Begin to boil a large pot of water. Start cooking noodles when the water boils.

3. As soon as the eggplant is soft, proceed with recipe. Drain and rinse the noodles when they are *al dente*; return to pot and toss with oil.

4. Serve the noodles on warm plates; top with Eggplant Szechuan. Garnish with green onions. Toss Mung Bean Salad. Serve.

Mung Bean, Green Onion and Sesame Seed Salad

2 cups mung bean sprouts, rinsed under cold running water and well drained

2 tablespoons chopped parsley or cilantro

1 tablespoon chopped fresh chives

3 green onions, thinly sliced

2 tablespoons toasted sesame seeds

DRESSING

1 teaspoon soy sauce

2 tablespoons lemon juice or rice vinegar

2 tablespoons vegetable oil

small pinch of anise seeds (optional)

Mix the ingredients for the dressing in a bowl large enough to hold the salad. Put the remaining ingredients into the bowl. Cover and chill. Toss just before serving.

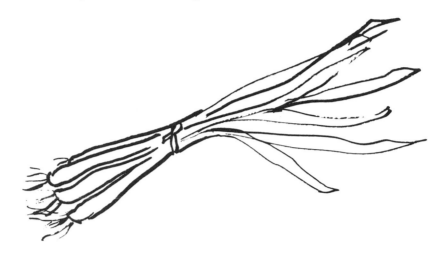

Eggplant Szechuan with Buckwheat Noodles

1 medium-sized eggplant

2 tablespoons vegetable oil

8 oz. buckwheat noodles or other noodles

1 tablespoon finely chopped or grated ginger root

4 cloves garlic, finely minced

¼ teaspoon (scant) dried red pepper flakes

2 teaspoons Chinese black bean paste (don't substitute miso)

1 teaspoon soy sauce

1 teaspoon sugar

½ cup chicken stock or water

2 teaspoons Chinese sesame oil

2 teaspoons Chinese dark vinegar

2 tablespoons chopped green onions

water on hand to add to eggplant

Cut the eggplant into thumb-sized pieces. Assemble all the other ingredients. Heat 2 tablespoons vegetable oil and sauté the eggplant over medium low heat. Keep the skillet covered between stirrings and add 2 tablespoons of water at a time if the eggplant sticks to the pan.

Boil a pot of water to cook the noodles. When the water boils, cook the noodles until they are *al dente*.

When the eggplant is very soft, transfer it to a bowl. Add a film of oil to the skillet; stir-fry the ginger, garlic, red pepper flakes and bean paste. Mix together the soy sauce, sugar, and stock or water; add to the skillet. Stir smooth and rapidly bring to a boil. Return the eggplant to the skillet and cook 1 minute longer. Sprinkle with sesame oil and vinegar. Toss.

The cooked noodles should be drained in a colander, rinsed under very warm water and shaken to remove the excess water. Return to pot and toss with 1 teaspoon sesame oil.

Serve the noodles on warm plates. Top with the eggplant; garnish each serving with green onions.

Fettucine with Herbed Spinach
Simple Waldorf Salad
Garlic Bread

SERVES 2

(easily doubled)

TIME TO PREPARE

30 minutes

INGREDIENTS

ON HAND

- ☐ *butter*
- ☐ *fresh garlic*
- ☐ *fresh or dried oregano*
- ☐ *fresh or dried basil*
- ☐ *nutmeg*
- ☐ *Parmesan cheese*
- ☐ *paprika*

SHOPPING LIST

- ☐ *1 10-oz. package frozen chopped spinach*
- ☐ *8 oz. fettucine noodles*
- ☐ *1 yellow onion or 2 shallots*
- ☐ *fresh parsley*
- ☐ *2 red-skinned apples*
- ☐ *celery (you need only 2 small stalks)*
- ☐ *¼ cup broken walnut meat*
- ☐ *8 oz. plain low-fat yogurt*
- ☐ *1 loaf French bread or whole wheat sour dough*
- ☐ *3 slices bacon or soy "Baco-bits" (optional)*

OVERVIEW

1. Prepare the Waldorf Salad and chill until serving.

2. Prepare Garlic Bread and place in a 350° oven.

3. Prepare fettucine dish.

Simple Waldorf Salad

2 small apples, diced

2 medium stalks of celery, diced

¼ cup broken walnut meat

½ to 1 cup plain low-fat yogurt

Combine ingredients, adding the amount of yogurt that seems right to you. Chill until serving.

Garlic Bread

See instructions on page 34. Put the garlic bread into a 350° oven before beginning the fettucine dish.

Fettucine with Herbed Spinach

1 10-oz. package frozen chopped spinach

8 oz. fettucine

3 tablespoons butter

1 yellow onion or 2 shallots, minced

2 tablespoons chopped fresh parsley

½ teaspoon dried basil or 1 teaspoon minced fresh basil

½ teaspoon dried oregano or 1 teaspoon minced fresh oregano

¼ teaspoon nutmeg

salt and freshly ground pepper to taste

freshly grated Parmesan cheese to pass at the table

OPTIONAL GARNISH

3 slices of crisp-fried bacon, crumbled, or soy "Baco-bits"

Thaw the spinach by placing on a trivet over boiling water. (You want to be able to just fork it apart, not cook it.) Begin to boil a pot of water in which to cook the noodles. While preparing the spinach mixture, cook the noodles until *al dente.*

Transfer the spinach to a food processor with the metal blade in place, or a blender. Melt 3 tablespoons butter in a skillet; sauté the onion or shallots until golden. Transfer to the processor; add the herbs and purée.

When the noodles are cooked, gently warm the spinach mixture over low heat. In a colander, drain and rinse the noodles, then shake off excess moisture. Stir the noodles into the herbed spinach mixture. Adjust seasonings. Serve on warm plates. Garnish with crumbled bacon or "Baco-bits," if desired, and pass grated Parmesan at the table.

Unusual Creamy Seaweed Soup
Crisp Ginger Carrots

SERVES 2

TIME TO PREPARE

25 minutes

INGREDIENTS

ON HAND
- ☐ *white vinegar*
- ☐ *soy sauce*
- ☐ *honey or sugar*
- ☐ *fresh ginger*
- ☐ *fresh garlic*
- ☐ *cayenne*

SHOPPING LIST
- ☐ *tahini (sesame butter) or any kind of smooth nut butter*
- ☐ *1 15-oz. can garbanzo beans or 2 cups homecooked garbanzo beans*
- ☐ *1 bunch watercress*
- ☐ *2 medium-sized carrots*
- ☐ *¼ cup seaweed (*wakame *or* kombu, *for example)*
- ☐ *fresh parsley*

Rain constantly washes the earth's minerals into the sea; these minerals are taken up by the life in the sea and become abundantly available to us through seaweed. Seaweed is a terrific source of trace minerals, the same minerals which are absent in land-grown vegetables cultivated in chemically pumped up, organically depleted soil.

You can reduce the high sodium level in seaweed by rinsing it in cold tap water. The white powder on its surface includes most of the sodium.

OVERVIEW

1. Begin by making the Carrot Salad.

2. Move on to preparing the soup.

Crisp Ginger Carrots

2 medium-sized carrots

¼ cup white vinegar

1 tablespoon sugar or 2 teaspoons honey

2 teaspoons water

2 teaspoons soy sauce

2 teaspoons grated fresh ginger*

Peel the carrots; cut them into 2-inch lengths and then each length into skinny strips. Scatter the cut–up carrot on a clean dish towel. Lightly salt. Let sit for about 15 minutes. Squeeze the carrot strips in the towel to remove the moisture. In a bowl, stir together the remaining ingredients; add the carrots and toss. Carrots prepared this way will store for several days in the refrigerator and make a healthful, delicious palate cleanser. For variation, use half daikon radish and half carrot.

*Store your fresh ginger in the freezer. It won't mold or go soft and you can very easily grate it into a fine mash using a coarse-sized grater.

Unusual Creamy Seaweed Soup

¼ cup seaweed snipped into small pieces with kitchen scissors

¼ cup parsley, stems removed

1 bunch watercress, stems removed

1 15-oz. can garbanzo beans, drained or 2 cups homecooked garbanzo beans

¼ cup tahini (sesame butter) or any smooth nut butter

2 cloves garlic, pressed

2 ½ cups water

dash cayenne

Steam the seaweed, parsley and watercress over 2 cups water for 5 minutes. Purée the beans, steamed vegetables, steaming water, tahini and garlic. Return to saucepan. Add ½ cup water to the processor or blender and swish clean, then add this water to the soup. Warm gently, stirring in more water if necessary. Do not bring to a boil. Taste for seasonings; add cayenne and salt if desired.

Pasta Primavera

Tossed Greens with Vinaigrette Dressing

Garlic Bread

SERVES 6

TIME TO PREPARE

60 minutes

INGREDIENTS

ON HAND
- [ ] *salad oil*
- [ ] *red wine vinegar*
- [ ] *Dijon-type mustard*
- [ ] *butter*
- [ ] *fresh garlic*
- [ ] *rosemary*
- [ ] *fresh or dried basil*
- [ ] *paprika*

SHOPPING LIST
- [ ] *1 lb. spaghetti or vermicelli*
- [ ] *½ pint heavy cream*
- [ ] *¼ lb. sweet butter*
- [ ] *½ lb. Parmesan cheese*
- [ ] *½ cup shelled sunflower seeds or pine nuts*
- [ ] *16 cherry tomatoes*
- [ ] *½ lb. fresh mushrooms*
- [ ] *8 to 12 spears fresh asparagus*
- [ ] *2 lbs. fresh peas*
- [ ] *3 small zucchini*
- [ ] *fresh parsley*
- [ ] *crisp dark greens for 6*
- [ ] *1 loaf French bread*

The poet Rainer Maria Rilke once said something like this: "I am vast; therefore I encompass contradictions." Including Pasta Primavera in this cookbook is a contradiction; delicately steamed vegetables are lavished with cream and butter and cheese. It is wonderful.

OVERVIEW

1. Assemble the equipment to make Pasta Primavera.

2. Prepare the salad dressing and greens. (*See page 100 for Vinaigrette Dressings.*) Cover and chill the salad greens until ready to toss with dressing and serve.

3. Prepare the Garlic Bread. (*See page 34 for instructions.*) Preheat oven to 350°.

4. Prepare Pasta Primavera. Halfway through, pop the bread in the oven to warm.

Pasta Primavera

½ lb. Parmesan cheese

1 lb. vermicelli or spaghetti

3 small zucchini, sliced on the diagonal into ¼-inch slices

2 lbs. fresh peas, shelled

8 to 12 spears fresh asparagus, tough ends removed, sliced on the diagonal into 1-inch lengths

16 cherry tomatoes, cut in half

¼ cup sweet butter or olive oil

½ cup shelled sunflower seeds or pine nuts

4 or 5 cloves garlic, pressed

½ lb. fresh mushrooms, sliced

¼ cup finely chopped parsley

¼ cup fresh minced basil or 3 to 4 tablespoons dried basil

½ teaspoon crushed dried rosemary

½ pint heavy cream

1 tablespoon sweet butter

salt and freshly ground pepper to taste

The key to preparing this dish is having everything ready and at hand before you begin cooking. You'll need:
- a large pot with salted water to cook the pasta
- a pot and steaming trivet to steam the vegetables
- a large skillet to sauté the mushrooms and reheat the vegetables
- a small saucepan to warm the cream
- a bowl to hold the steamed vegetables
- paper towels to drain the sautéed sunseeds or pinenuts
- a garlic press and 4 to 5 cloves garlic, peeled
- a slotted spoon, a large spoon for stirring, and a colander

Grate the Parmesan and prepare all the vegetables for steaming. Steam the asparagus, zucchini and peas separately so that they are perfectly tender-crisp. Transfer them to a bowl as they finish steaming. Put the sliced cherry tomatoes in this bowl, too. Begin boiling the water for the pasta.

Heat ¼ cup sweet butter (or olive oil) in a large, heavy skillet. Sauté the sunseeds or pine nuts until slightly browned. Remove from the pan with a slotted spoon and drain on paper towels. Add the pressed garlic, mushrooms and herbs to the skillet. Stir gently until the mushrooms are tender. Add the pasta to the boiling water.

On very low heat, warm the steamed vegetables in the skillet with the mushrooms and herbs. Stir in the seeds or pine nuts. In a small saucepan, warm 1 cup cream with 1 tablespoon sweet butter. Bring to a simmer and stir in half of the Parmesan. Remove from heat.

When cooked *al dente*, pour the pasta into a colander. Rinse under hot running water, shake off excess moisture and return to pot. Toss with the cream-Parmesan mixture; add freshly ground black pepper and salt to taste. Gently add the vegetables to the pasta.

Serve on warm plates. Pass the remaining Parmesan cheese around the table.

Garlic Bread

See instructions on page 34. Preheat oven to 350° when you begin preparation of Pasta Primavera. Heat the garlic bread when the pasta dish is halfway done.

Tossed Green Salad with Vinaigrette Dressing

See page 100 for instructions

Sicilian Eggplant
Cracked Wheat or Bulgur
Tossed Greens with Vinaigrette Dressing

SERVES 4

TIME TO PREPARE

40 minutes

INGREDIENTS

ON HAND
- [ ] *cracked wheat or bulgur*
- [ ] *olive oil*
- [ ] *red wine vinegar*
- [ ] *fresh garlic*
- [ ] *basil*
- [ ] *2 ¼ cups vegetable broth or chicken stock (optional)*

SHOPPING LIST
- [ ] *1 28-oz. can whole peeled tomatoes*
- [ ] *12 Sicilian or Greek olives*
- [ ] *capers (2 tablespoons)*
- [ ] *2 small or 1 large eggplant*
- [ ] *2 oz. pine nuts or sunflower seeds*
- [ ] *2 oz. Parmesan or dry Jack cheese*
- [ ] *2 red bell peppers (use green if red peppers are unavailable)*
- [ ] *celery*
- [ ] *1 small yellow onion*
- [ ] *salad greens for 4*
- [ ] *fresh parsley*

This eggplant dish has a rich "meaty" taste. The next day it makes a wonderful lunch and needn't be reheated, but it's more savory at room temperature than refrigerator cold.

Sicilian Eggplant uses a fair amount of capers which are rather expensive. A quite acceptable substitute is pickled nasturtium seeds. They keep as well as capers, the ingredients cost next to nothing, and they are simple to make. Here's a recipe:

Pickled Nasturtium Seeds

2 ½ cups cider or white vinegar	1 small chopped onion
¼ cup peppercorns	1 bay leaf

Place the ingredients in a saucepan. Bring to a boil and simmer 5 minutes. Pour into a bowl, cover and cool. Strain into a jar. As the nasturtium flowers lose their petals, gather the seed pods (while still very small) and put into the vinegar mixture. Cover and keep in a cool place; allow the seeds to cure 30 days before eating.

OVERVIEW

1. Begin cooking the cracked wheat.

2. Prepare the eggplant dish.

3. While the eggplant simmers, prepare the salad and dressing. (*See page 100 for Vinaigrette Dressings.*) Cover and chill salad greens until ready to toss with dressing and serve.

Cracked Wheat or Bulgur

1   tablespoon olive oil

1   small yellow onion, chopped

1 ½   cups bulgur or cracked wheat

2 ¼   cups water, vegetable broth or chicken stock

Warm the oil in a skillet or pot with a tight-fitting lid. Over medium high heat, sauté the onion and cracked wheat until the wheat is toasted, or about 3 to 5 minutes. Stir constantly. Add the liquid, cover and bring to a boil. Simmer over very low heat until the liquid is absorbed (15 to 20 minutes for bulgur; about 25 minutes for cracked wheat).

Sicilian Eggplant

¼   cup olive oil

4   cloves garlic, minced

4   to 5 inner stalks of celery, sliced thin

2   oz. pine nuts or sunflower seeds (2 tablespoons)

2   small or 1 large eggplant, cut into thumb-sized pieces

1   28-oz. can whole peeled tomatoes, drained

2   bell peppers, diced

12   Sicilian or Greek olives, pitted and coarsely chopped

2   tablespoons capers or pickled nasturtium seeds (at left)

4   tablespoons minced fresh basil or 2 tablespoons dried basil

¼   teaspoon freshly ground pepper

1   tablespoon chopped fresh parsley

½   cup freshly grated Parmesan cheese or dry Jack

Heat the olive oil in a heavy skillet with a lid. Over medium high heat, sauté the garlic and celery until the celery is soft. Stir in the pine nuts or sunflower seeds and eggplant. Stir until the eggplant is coated with oil. Add the tomatoes, breaking them up in the skillet with a large spoon. Stir in the bell peppers, olives, capers, basil and black pepper. Cover and simmer 15 minutes.

Uncover and stir in the parsley. Taste the eggplant; continue cooking until the eggplant is thoroughly soft.

Serve over cracked wheat. Generously sprinkle with grated cheese and garnish with chopped parsley. Pass extra grated cheese around the table.

Tossed Green Salad with Vinaigrette Dressing

See page 100 for instructions

Herbed Mushrooms and Eggs
Greek Salad
Warmed Pita or Crusty Bread

SERVES 4

TIME TO PREPARE

20 minutes

INGREDIENTS

ON HAND
- ☐ *8 eggs*
- ☐ *butter*
- ☐ *olive oil*
- ☐ *soy sauce*
- ☐ *red wine vinegar*
- ☐ *fresh or dried tarragon*
- ☐ *dry mustard*

SHOPPING LIST
- ☐ *4 oz. feta cheese*
- ☐ *12 green or Greek olives*
- ☐ *½ lb. fresh mushrooms*
- ☐ *1 head Romaine lettuce*
- ☐ *1 small red onion*
- ☐ *1 medium-sized cucumber*
- ☐ *2 medium-sized tomatoes*
- ☐ *pita or crusty bread*

This meal is especially pleasant when you are exhausted or pressed for time. With minimal effort, you'll create a meal pleasing to the eye with complicated tastes and textures that tantalize the tongue and satisfy the appetite.

Greece. Brilliant white sunlight reflected upon bare limestone cliffs. Dusty roads lined with olive trees. This vision of the Greek landscape seems eternal, but actually it began in the 6th century B.C. when Solon's Edict made illegal the exportation of any Greek agricultural product except for olive oil. In response, farmers tore out other crops and trees in order to plant olives. Unfortunately, olive trees have long tap roots that fail to prevent the erosion of topsoil. The Greek landscape totally transformed. By the 4th century B.C., Plato was lamenting the loss of the green meadows, woodlands and springs that had been the Attic countryside.

The exportation of olive oil made Athens rich, for in the ancient world, oil was used not only for food but also for lighting, in purification rituals, as a perfumed unguent and in the preparation of medicine. Athens, however, became unable to provide its people with basic food supplies because the raising of livestock and grain had virtually disappeared. Greece found itself in the position of having to expand its empire to feed its people.

OVERVIEW

1. Place the bread in the oven to heat, unless you plan to toast it later. Slice the mushrooms; sauté in butter and tarragon. Beat the eggs lightly with the soy sauce.

2. Assemble the salad.

3. Prepare the Herbed Mushrooms and Eggs. (If you want to toast bread rather than heat it in the oven, pop it in the toaster now.)

4. Dress and toss the salad. Serve.

Greek Salad

1 head, or about ¾ lb. Romaine lettuce

2 tomatoes, cut up

1 small red onion, sliced into thin rings

1 medium-sized cucumber, sliced thin

4 oz. feta cheese, crumbled

12 green olives, halved or sliced or 12 Greek olives, pitted and chopped

DRESSING

2 tablespoons olive oil

1 tablespoon plus 1 teaspoon red wine vinegar

a robust dash of dry mustard

freshly ground pepper

Whisk together the dressing ingredients on the bottom of the salad bowl. Tear the lettuce into the bowl and top with the rest of the ingredients. Toss just before serving.

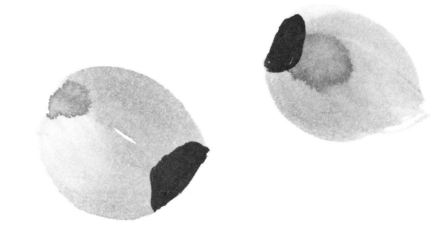

Herbed Mushrooms and Eggs

½ lb. fresh mushrooms, sliced

1 tablespoon butter

1 teaspoon dried tarragon or 2 teaspoons minced fresh tarragon

8 eggs*

½ teaspoon soy sauce

salt and freshly ground pepper to taste

Sauté the mushrooms in butter with the tarragon, stirring to coat the mushrooms with melted butter. Cover and cook 5 minutes over medium heat. Turn the heat very low until you are ready to cook the eggs. Beat the eggs with the soy sauce. Raise heat slightly. Pour eggs over the mushrooms and cook slowly, stirring frequently. Season with salt and pepper to taste. Serve.

*To reduce cholesterol intake, use 4 whole eggs and 8 egg whites. Or substitute 7 ½ oz. tofu cut into ¾-inch cubes for 4 of the eggs; stir the cubed tofu into the beaten eggs. Increase the amount of soy sauce to 1 teaspoon. Pour over the sautéed mushrooms and stir gently until the eggs are cooked.

Sautéed Broccoli with Pasta

Fennel and Red Radish Salad

SERVINGS

2 large or 4 small

TIME TO PREPARE

30 minutes

INGREDIENTS

ON HAND

- ☐ *olive oil*
- ☐ *red wine vinegar*
- ☐ *Dijon-type mustard*
- ☐ *fresh garlic*
- ☐ *basil*
- ☐ *oregano*

SHOPPING LIST

- ☐ *8 oz. noodles*
- ☐ *1 16-oz. can whole peeled tomatoes*
- ☐ *1 bunch broccoli*
- ☐ *4 green onions*
- ☐ *celery (only 1 stalk is needed)*
- ☐ *fresh parsley*
- ☐ *1 fennel bulb*
- ☐ *15 red radishes*
- ☐ *3 oz. freshly grated Parmesan, Romano or dried Jack cheese*

Sautéed broccoli can also be served with steamed new potatoes, rice or cracked wheat, rather than pasta; the results will be equally good. Fresh fennel, or *finocchio*, is available in late autumn and winter, as is anise, which can be substituted for fennel in the following recipe. Both look quite a bit like celery but have a softer, less stringy texture and a delicately sweet licorice taste. If you have a food processor, use it to very thinly slice the fennel and radishes quickly and efficiently.

OVERVIEW

1. Prepare fennel salad. Refrigerate until serving.

2. Begin boiling water for pasta. Prepare vegetables for pasta dish.

3. Prepare pasta dish.

Fennel and Red Radish Salad

3 tablespoons olive oil

1 tablespoon red wine vinegar

1 teaspoon Dijon-type mustard

⅛ teaspoon salt

½ cup minced parsley

1 fennel bulb

15 red radishes

freshly ground pepper to taste

Combine the olive oil, vinegar, mustard, salt and parsley in the bottom of your salad bowl. Remove the upper stalks and tough outer layer of the fennel bulb. Slice off the tough bottom core. Slice the remaining bulb as thin as possible, removing any tough portion of the core which may remain. Add to the salad bowl. Slice the radishes as thin as possible; add to salad bowl and toss. Add freshly ground pepper to taste and chill until serving.

Serve in individual rice bowls alongside the sautéed broccoli dish.

Sautéed Broccoli with Pasta

8 oz. noodles

2 tablespoons olive oil

4 green onions, thinly sliced

2 to 4 cloves garlic, minced

1 stalk celery, chopped

1 16-oz. can whole peeled tomatoes, drained

1 teaspoon dried basil or 2 teaspoons minced fresh basil

1 teaspoon dried oregano or 2 teaspoons minced fresh oregano

1 bunch broccoli

3 oz. freshly grated Parmesan, Romano or dried Jack cheese

3 tablespoons minced parsley

Begin to boil a pot of water to cook the noodles. Prepare the broccoli: cut off and divide flowerets; peel the tough outer skin from the stem and cut into bite-sized pieces.

Heat 2 tablespoons olive oil in a large skillet. Sauté the onions, garlic and celery for 2 to 3 minutes, or until soft. Add the tomatoes and herbs; break the tomatoes up in the skillet with a large spoon.

Cover the skillet and simmer 5 minutes. Stir in the broccoli; cover and simmer for approximately 8 minutes, or until the broccoli is just tender. Start cooking the pasta. Stir the grated cheese and parsley into the broccoli. Cook uncovered over low heat for 5 minutes. Salt and pepper to taste.

When the noodles are cooked *al dente*, drain them in a colander and rinse under hot water. Shake off excess moisture. Return to pot and toss with a little butter or olive oil, if desired. Serve the broccoli and sauce on a bed of noodles. Pass extra grated cheese around the table.

Pasta Salad
Chilled Melon Slices
Warm Crusty Bread

SERVES 2

(easily increased)

TIME TO PREPARE

30 minutes

INGREDIENTS

ON HAND
- ☐ *olive oil*
- ☐ *white wine vinegar*
- ☐ *fresh garlic*
- ☐ *Parmesan cheese*

SHOPPING LIST
- ☐ *8 oz. green fettucine*
- ☐ *1 bunch broccoli*
- ☐ *1 small red onion*
- ☐ *12 cherry tomatoes*
- ☐ *1 melon (honeydew, cantaloupe, etc.)*
- ☐ *2 oz. Jarlsberg cheese*
- ☐ *16 Greek olives*
- ☐ *⅓ lb. prosciutto or "deli" ham, sliced very thin (optional)*
- ☐ *1 loaf of crusty bread*

It is said that Marco Polo introduced pasta into Italy by bringing back noodles from China. Current Italian law requires that pasta be made with durum wheat and water only, without artificial preservatives, flavors or colorings. Egg pasta must have five fresh whole eggs for every two pounds of flour. In the U.S., pasta is also made from durum wheat, but the flour is more refined so it is fortified with minerals and vitamins. Egg noodles are usually made with frozen eggs or powdered eggs.

OVERVIEW

1. Cut up melon and chill.

2. Begin to boil water to cook pasta.

3. Wrap bread in aluminum foil and place in 275° oven.

4. Prepare the pasta salad.

Pasta Salad

DRESSING

½ *cup olive oil*

4 *tablespoons white wine vinegar*

2 *cloves garlic, pressed*

1 *bunch broccoli*

8 *oz. green fettucine*

12 *cherry tomatoes*

16 *Greek olives*

1 *small red onion*

⅓ *lb. prosciutto or "deli" ham (optional)*

2 *oz. Jarlsberg cheese*

freshly grated Parmesan cheese

Begin to boil a pot of water. Measure the ingredients for the dressing into a covered jar; shake and set aside.

Cut up the broccoli; measure out 2 cups flowerets. (Use the rest in soup or a stir-fry dish.) Prepare a bowl of ice water. Toss the flowerets into the boiling water and leave for 10 seconds, or until they are bright green. Scoop them out with a strainer or slotted spoon and transfer to the ice water. Leave in the ice water until thoroughly cooled. Drain well and place in a large bowl. Toss with half the dressing. Set aside.

Add salt and 1 tablespoon olive oil to the boiling water and begin cooking the fettucine. Slice the tomatoes in half and pit the olives; toss with the broccoli.

Slice the onion and optional prosciutto or ham; cut the Jarlsberg cheese into small cubes. Make sure you don't overcook the pasta! When the pasta is *al dente*, drain and rinse the noodles under cold water. Drain well and transfer to a salad bowl, preferably a broad, shallow one. Immediately toss with the remaining dressing. Add the sliced onion, prosciutto or ham and Jarlsberg cheese; toss again. Ring with the broccoli, tomatoes and olives. Sprinkle the pasta generously with freshly grated Parmesan. Serve at room temperature.

Tofu

That tasteless, colorless blob of "But what do you do with it?" dismissed by many as leftover pie-in-the-sky from the '60s. Actually, it is a healthful, inexpensive source of complete protein—the primary source of protein for over a billion people on this planet. One of the primary reasons tofu is considered "health food" is that, unlike most sources of complete protein (whole eggs, dairy products and meat, for example), tofu is cholesterol-free. And 8 ounces of tofu provides 27% of an adult male's daily protein requirement but has only one-third the calories of 8 ounces of eggs, or one-fourth the calories of an 8-ounce steak.

Tofu is "soybean cheese." It is made by first soaking soybeans in water and then puréeing them. This mash is stirred into hot water and boiled, then strained. The soybean "milk" is simmered, then a coagulating agent is added. This is either nigari (the mineral byproduct left over when salt is evaporated from ocean water), or gypsum (calcium sulfate). With the addition of the coagulant, the soy milk separates into curds and whey. The cloud-white, custard-like, protein-rich and easily-digested curds are then pressed into small blocks. Of tofu.

So what do you do with it? The menus on pages 72 to 76 cast tofu in its characteristic role—a nurturing, substantive, but silent ingredient.

Tempeh

Although the scientific community has written more about tempeh than any other soybean food, tempeh is still largely unknown to people in the United States. Tempeh is very different from tofu in taste, texture and appearance. It comes in ¾-inch thick sheets, is as cratered and craggy as the surface of the moon, and is made from a fermentation process that utilizes the entire soybean. Tempeh can be made entirely from soybeans or may include other legumes, grains or seeds.

Tempeh is like tofu in that it is a terrific source of usable protein that does not have the negative effects of high cholesterol or chemical toxins (19.5% of tempeh is usable protein, which compares favorably to chicken, for example—21% of which is usable protein). Tempeh has the additional benefits of being a whole food, supplying plenty of fiber, and being the world's richest source of Vitamin B/12, which is known to be lacking in vegetarian diets.

As with yogurt, bread, beer and cheese, much of tempeh's appealing taste and texture can be attributed to the fermentation process. In The Book of Tempeh, *authors William Shurtleff and Akiko Aoyagi report that tempeh's "subtly sweet, fresh aroma" has been described as "'nutty,' 'cheesey,' 'mushroomy,' or 'yeasty, like freshly baked bread.'" The primary advantage of tempeh over tofu, however, is culinary. Because of its firm texture, it can easily substitute for veal and chicken in a variety of delicious traditional recipes.*

Tempeh is available in health food stores and can be purchased frozen, packaged and refrigerated, or, if you live close to a tempeh-maker, fresh. Cost-wise, commercial tempeh is less expensive than fish or chicken.

The recipes on pages 78 to 81 will entice you to try tempeh. When you see the possibilities of this new ingredient, you may want to read the professional edition of The Book of Tempeh, *which I was able to get through my local library. It is, on many levels, a fascinating and wonderful book.*

Curry with Peppers, Tofu and Cashews

Dal or Rice

Cucumber Raita

SERVES 5

TIME TO PREPARE

50 minutes

INGREDIENTS

ON HAND

☐ *brown rice*

☐ *lentils, yellow split peas or mung beans**

☐ *sesame oil (optional)*

☐ *vegetable oil*

☐ *butter*

☐ *1 green onion*

☐ *fresh garlic*

☐ *fresh or powdered ginger*

☐ *curry powder*

☐ *turmeric*

☐ *cayenne*

☐ *cumin seeds*

☐ *ground cumin*

☐ *ground coriander*

SHOPPING LIST

☐ *1 10-oz. package frozen peas*

☐ *12 oz. firm tofu*

☐ *8 oz. plain low-fat yogurt*

☐ *¾ cup raw cashews*

☐ *3 yellow onions*

☐ *2 red or green bell peppers*

☐ *1 large cucumber*

☐ *fresh parsley or cilantro*

☐ *1 lemon*

This menu includes two dishes with which you may not be familiar: *raita* and *dal*. *Raita* is a yogurt salad that is often served as part of an Indian meal, especially a vegetarian meal because the yogurt serves as a primary source of protein. Use a yogurt that is not "tangy" and that is fairly thick and rich-tasting (in India, yogurt is made from buffalo's milk, which makes a quite rich, almost cheese-like yogurt). Raitas are made with three different types of ingredients: raw vegetables as in this one; cooked vegetables; or dumplings, fruits and nuts to create elaborate, sweet raitas for celebrations.

Dal is simply the Indian word for legumes, so there are many different recipes for "dal." Often, it is prepared quite simply, as in the following recipe; the legumes are cooked with herbs and seasonings, then puréed and used as a dip for bread or served with rice.

*Red lentils are the quickest cooking lentils; they cook in ten minutes. Other lentils take 30 minutes.

OVERVIEW

1. Begin to cook 1 cup brown rice in 2 cups of water.

2. Prepare the Dal.

3. Prepare the Raita. Chill until serving.

4. Prepare the Curry with Peppers, Tofu, and Cashews.

Dal

1 cup dried lentils, yellow split peas or mung beans

2 cups water

1 teaspoon salt

½ teaspoon turmeric

⅛ to ¼ teaspoon cayenne

2 tablespoons sesame oil or 1 tablespoon butter plus 1 tablespoon vegetable oil

1 medium-sized yellow onion, thinly sliced

1 teaspoon cumin seeds

½ teaspoon ground coriander

Pick through the dried legumes to remove dirt and rocks; then rinse. Put the legumes, water, salt, turmeric, and cayenne in a pot with a tight-fitting lid. Bring to a boil; cover and simmer. Heat 2 tablespoons sesame oil (or 1 tablespoon vegetable oil plus 1 tablespoon butter) in a large heavy skillet. Over medium high heat, sauté the onion until it is softened and straw-colored. Add the cumin seeds and coriander; stir until the cumin turns dark brown. Add to the legumes. Simmer the legumes for a total of 30 minutes, or until they are tender. Dal is traditionally served rather dry; if you prefer a moister dal, stir in some water.

Cucumber Raita

1 large cucumber

8 oz. plain low-fat yogurt

1 tablespoon lemon juice

1 clove garlic, pressed

1 tablespoon minced parsley or cilantro

If the cucumber has large seeds, slice it lengthwise and scrape out the seeds. Peel and coarsely grate it. Combine all ingredients in a bowl; taste for seasonings. Chill.

1 teaspoon ground cumin

2 tablespoons chopped green onion

salt and freshly ground pepper to taste

Curry with Peppers, Tofu and Cashews

¾ cup raw cashew pieces

2 tablespoons vegetable oil

2 medium onions, peeled and sliced thin

1 tablespoon curry powder

2 cloves garlic, pressed

1 teaspoon salt

1 teaspoon grated fresh ginger or ½ teaspoon powdered ginger

¼ cup water

12 oz. firm tofu cut into 1-inch cubes

2 large green or red bell peppers, sliced into strips

1 10-oz. package frozen peas

Stir the cashews in a dry skillet over medium heat until they are lightly browned. They burn quickly, so don't leave them unattended. Remove from the pan and set aside.

Heat 2 tablespoons oil in the skillet. Sauté the onions over medium high heat. When they are soft, reduce the heat slightly and add the curry, garlic, salt and ginger. Stir. Add ¼ cup water to the skillet and gently stir in the tofu and peppers. Cover and cook 5 to 7 minutes. Add the peas and more water if you'd like. Cook for 2 minutes. Stir in the cashews and remove from heat. Keep covered until you are ready to serve.

Just Right Fried Rice
Hot and Sweet Cabbage Salad

SERVES 3

TIME TO PREPARE

20 minutes (with cooked rice on hand)

INGREDIENTS

ON HAND

- ☐ *2 cups cooked brown rice*
- ☐ *2 eggs*
- ☐ *vegetable oil*
- ☐ *Chinese sesame oil*
- ☐ *white, cider or rice vinegar*
- ☐ *honey*
- ☐ *sugar*
- ☐ *oyster sauce or soy sauce*
- ☐ *Tabasco*

SHOPPING LIST

- ☐ *12 oz. firm tofu or 1 thick slice of ham (¼ lb.) and 1 small can cooked shrimp*
- ☐ *1 10-oz. package frozen peas*
- ☐ *3 cups mung bean sprouts*
- ☐ *1 bunch green onions*
- ☐ *1 small Chinese cabbage (also called Napa cabbage) or 1 large, firm cucumber*

This meal is a medley of the Chinese concept of the Five Flavors: bitter, salt, sour, hot and sweet. One of the earliest known recipes for the ubiquitous Fried Rice dates back to the Han Era (202 B.C.–A.D. 220). Described in the *Li-Chi*, a book of rituals, rice was fried with the crisped fat of a wolf's breast and was one of the Eight Delicacies to be prepared for the elderly on ceremonial occasions.

Archaeological investigations show that rice was cultivated as early as 3500 B.C. in northern Thailand. By 2800 B.C. it was considered one of the Five Sacred Crops of China (along with wheat, barley, millet and soybeans). In India, rice is called "an immortal son of heaven;" 25% to 33% of that country's arable land is devoted to its cultivation.

Six out of ten people alive today rely upon rice as their primary source of food. Although rice was not introduced into Japan until the 1st century B.C., today the average intake of rice per person is one-half pound per day. In China, it is double that amount. Currently, Asia produces 90% of the world's rice crop but needs to import more than it can grow; however, only 5% of the world's rice crop is presently part of an import-export market.

OVERVIEW

1. Prepare the cabbage salad. Refrigerate until serving.

2. Prepare the fried rice.

3. Serve the cabbage salad in small individual bowls alongside the rice.

Hot and Sweet Cabbage Salad

1 small Chinese cabbage (also called Napa cabbage), or 1 large cucumber

1 teaspoon Chinese sesame oil

1 tablespoon cider, rice or white vinegar

1 tablespoon sugar

8 to 10 dashes Tabasco

½ teaspoon salt

Mix together the oil, vinegar, sugar, Tabasco and salt on the bottom of the salad bowl. Very thinly slice the cabbage. (If you are using cucumbers: peel and halve lengthwise; remove seeds and slice very thin.) Add to the salad bowl and toss; chill until serving.

Fried Rice

2 tablespoons vegetable oil

2 eggs, lightly beaten

2 cups cooked brown rice

½ cup frozen peas

2 cups firm tofu, cubed or ½ cup diced ham plus 1 small can cooked shrimp

2 tablespoons oyster sauce or 2 tablespoons soy sauce

3 cups mung bean sprouts

Heat 2 tablespoons oil in a heavy skillet or wok. Add the eggs; stir until cooked, breaking them up into small pieces. Add the rice, stirring quickly until it is thoroughly heated. Add the peas, tofu or ham and shrimp, and oyster sauce or soy sauce. Stir gently and continuously until the ingredients are well blended and thoroughly warm. Add the bean sprouts and toss the ingredients together for another 30 seconds. Sprinkle in the green onions and serve.

NOTE

You could add a variety of other ingredients to this basic recipe. Finely chopped celery or summer squash, grated carrot, sunflower seeds, sesame seeds, minced garlic and ginger are possible additions. Sauté any of these for a moment, add the lightly beaten eggs, then add the rice, etc.

Sweet and Sour Tofu
Pungent Greens
Rice

SERVES 2 TO 3

TIME TO PREPARE

30 minutes

INGREDIENTS

ON HAND
- [ ] *brown or converted rice*
- [ ] *vegetable oil*
- [ ] *Chinese sesame oil*
- [ ] *rice vinegar*
- [ ] *dry sherry*
- [ ] *catsup or tomato paste*
- [ ] *soy sauce*
- [ ] *honey*
- [ ] *fresh garlic*
- [ ] *fresh or powdered ginger*
- [ ] *cornstarch or arrowroot*
- [ ] *sesame seeds (optional garnish)*

SHOPPING LIST
- [ ] *1 20-oz. can pineapple chunks*
- [ ] *8 oz. firm tofu*
- [ ] *1 lb. greens (mustard, kale, beet greens, turnip greens, chard, etc.)*
- [ ] *5 green onions*
- [ ] *1 green bell pepper*
- [ ] *3 medium-sized tomatoes or 1 cup cherry tomatoes*

Glazed in the persimmon-colored sweet and sour sauce are chunks of yellow pineapple, white tofu and bright green pepper. A visual treat, this meal displays tofu in all its protein-rich but bland splendor—the perfect foil to the vibrant tastes and textures of a sweet and sour sauce.

OVERVIEW

1. If you precooked rice in the morning, complete cooking the rice now. With precooked rice (*see page 99 for directions*) this meal will take 30 minutes to cook. If you are starting rice from scratch it will take 45 to 50 minutes.

2. Prepare the sweet and sour sauce.

3. You will have to stir-fry the tofu dish and the greens in different skillets at the same time, so cut up the vegetables and assemble all the ingredients for both dishes beforehand.

4. Begin cooking the tofu dish. When you add the sweet and sour sauce to the tofu, begin to stir-fry the greens in another skillet. The greens will take approximately 5 minutes to cook.

Sweet and Sour Tofu

SWEET AND SOUR SAUCE

2 ½ tablespoons honey

4 tablespoons rice vinegar

3 tablespoons soy sauce

2 tablespoons tomato paste or catsup

½ teaspoon grated fresh ginger or 1 teaspoon powdered ginger

1 tablespoon arrowroot or cornstarch

1 20-oz. can pineapple chunks

½ cup pineapple juice (reserved after draining pineapple)

2 tablespoons vegetable oil

5 green onions

1 clove garlic, pressed

1 green bell pepper

3 medium-sized tomatoes or 1 cup cherry tomatoes

8 oz. firm tofu

Drain the juice from the pineapple, reserving ½ cup for the sauce. Combine the ingredients for the sweet and sour sauce, stirring in the chunks of pineapple last, and set aside.

Prepare the vegetables: cut the green onions into 2-inch lengths, fresh stems included; cut the green pepper into 1-inch squares; dice medium-sized tomatoes or halve cherry tomatoes. Cut the tofu into ¾-inch cubes.

Heat 2 tablespoons oil in a large skillet. Add the onions and stir-fry over medium high heat until slightly softened. Reduce heat to medium and stir in garlic, green pepper and tomatoes. Stir in the sweet and sour sauce. Simmer, stirring frequently, until thickened. Stir in the tofu carefully and continue cooking over a low heat until it is just heated through. (Do not overcook a sauce that is thickened with cornstarch; it will get thin again.)

Pungent Greens

2 teaspoons vegetable oil

2 cloves garlic, peeled and thinly sliced

1 lb. fresh greens (kale, chard, spinach, beet greens, collards) washed, tough stems removed and coarsely chopped

2 tablespoons dry sherry

Chinese sesame oil

toasted sesame seeds (optional garnish)

To toast the sesame seeds, put them in a dry skillet over medium heat. When you begin to smell their roasted aroma and they begin to pop, stir until they are golden brown. Remove from skillet and set aside. An easier method is to toast seeds (and nuts) in a toaster oven if you have one.

Heat vegetable oil in a large skillet or pot with a tight-fitting lid. Stir-fry the garlic until it is browned, then remove from skillet. Add the greens and sherry, stir and cover. Cook over medium heat until the greens are tender but still slightly chewy (about 5 minutes). Dribble a little sesame oil over each serving and sprinkle with toasted sesame seeds.

Tempeh, Mushroom and Artichoke Hearts Sauté

Couscous

Brussels Sprouts

SERVES 2 TO 3

TIME TO PREPARE

20 minutes

INGREDIENTS

ON HAND

☐ *flour*
☐ *white wine*
☐ *butter*
☐ *vegetable bouillon cube or chicken broth (½ cup)*
☐ *nutmeg*

SHOPPING LIST

☐ *8 oz. tempeh*
☐ *1 cup couscous*
☐ *1 8-oz. can artichokes, waterpacked*
☐ *1 lemon*
☐ *18 Brussels sprouts*
☐ *10 fresh mushrooms*
☐ *1 oz. pine nuts (optional)*

You'll want to crisp and brown tempeh before you use it in a recipe. In this recipe, the tempeh is floured and browned in a little butter in a skillet; the flour serves to slightly thicken the sauce. In the next tempeh recipe, a different, quicker method is suggested that doesn't include flour.

OVERVIEW

1. Toast pine nuts, if desired.

2. Begin to brown tempeh.

3. Prepare the Brussels sprouts for cooking; begin steaming them.

4. Begin to boil water for couscous.

5. Continue preparing the tempeh dish. When you finish sautéeing the mushrooms, pour the boiling water over the couscous.

6. Complete preparation of the tempeh dish; cover and remove from heat. Complete the preparation of the Brussels sprouts.

Tempeh, Mushroom and Artichoke Hearts Sauté

8 oz. tempeh

flour

1 tablespoon butter

10 fresh mushrooms, sliced

1 8-oz. can water-packed artichoke hearts, drained

1 vegetable bouillon cube dissolved in ½ cup boiling water or ½ cup chicken broth

¼ cup white wine

juice of ½ lemon

freshly ground pepper to taste

Slice tempeh into narrow strips 2 to 3 inches long. Shake in plastic bag with flour so that they are well dusted. Melt 1 tablespoon butter in heavy skillet and very lightly fry the tempeh on both sides. The frying pan will be fairly dry when you turn the tempeh to the second side. Don't worry; it won't stick to the pan.

Remove the tempeh from the skillet. Sauté the mushrooms in the skillet with a little wine for 1 to 2 minutes. Stir into the skillet the remaining wine, bouillon or broth, drained artichoke hearts, lemon juice and ground pepper. Over high heat, reduce the liquid a bit. Lower heat and stir in the tempeh. The liquid will thicken slightly because of the flour on the tempeh. Cover and remove from heat. Serve over grains.

Couscous

1 cup couscous

1 cup boiling water

4 teaspoons toasted pine nuts (optional)

Lightly toast the pine nuts in a dry, warm skillet, stirring constantly. Remove from skillet when slightly golden and set aside.

The ratio for cooking couscous is 1 part water to 1 part grain. Three quarters of a cup of dry couscous provides a generous serving for two people. Simply boil the water, stir in the couscous and optional pine nuts, cover and remove from the heat. Let sit for 5 minutes; fluff with chopsticks or fork just before serving.

Brussels Sprouts

18 Brussels sprouts

1 tablespoon butter

⅛ teaspoon nutmeg

salt and freshly ground pepper to taste

Rinse and remove discolored outer leaves of Brussels sprouts. Trim the stems and incise X's into them. In a heavy, tightly-covered pot, set the sprouts on a trivet over water. Steam for 15 minutes, or until the tip of a knife easily pierces the stems. (Check intermittently for doneness. If the sprouts are tender before you have completed cooking the tempeh dish, remove from heat and cock the cover to allow the steam to escape.)

Lift out the sprouts and trivet; drain the pot. Melt the butter in the pot; return the sprouts. Sprinkle them with salt, pepper and nutmeg and stir until the butter and spices are evenly distributed. Serve.

Tempeh Scallopini

Spaghetti Squash

Cauliflower with Lemon and Green Onion

SERVES 3

TIME TO PREPARE

30 minutes

INGREDIENTS

ON HAND
- ☐ *olive oil*
- ☐ *butter*
- ☐ *Sercial (dry) Madeira or dry sherry*
- ☐ *fresh garlic*
- ☐ *1 green onion*
- ☐ *basil*
- ☐ *Parmesan cheese*

SHOPPING LIST
- ☐ *8 oz. tempeh*
- ☐ *1 16-oz. can whole peeled tomatoes*
- ☐ *½ lb. fresh mushrooms*
- ☐ *1 small spaghetti squash*
- ☐ *1 head of cauliflower*
- ☐ *fresh parsley*
- ☐ *1 lemon*

This tempeh recipe incorporates the fastest way to crisp and brown the surface of tempeh: brushing the surface with a bit of olive oil and broiling it on each side for a few minutes.

Spaghetti squash is available in supermarkets when winter squashes such as acorn and butternut appear—late summer through winter. It is almost as easy to grow as zucchini, however, and the seeds are available through most major seed companies. This vegetable makes a wonderful alternative to grains or noodles and because of its hard shell doesn't need to be stored in the refrigerator. Spaghetti squash is delicious simply steamed and served with a little butter, salt and pepper, or it can be baked with any stuffing you would use with zucchini, bell peppers or eggplant.

OVERVIEW

1. Begin to steam the spaghetti squash.

2. Prepare the Tempeh Scallopini. Before adding the tempeh to the sauce, begin to cook the cauliflower.

Spaghetti Squash

With a large knife, remove stem end of squash, set on end and slice lengthwise in half. Scrape out the seeds. Steam on a trivet set in a large pot. Depending on the size of the squash and how the pieces fit in the pot, the squash will take 20 to 30 minutes to cook. Test softness with the tip of a knife. When the squash is cooked, scrape the flesh lengthwise with a fork. It will transform into thin spaghetti-like strands.

Tempeh Scallopini

1 tablespoon butter

½ lb. fresh mushrooms

1 clove garlic, pressed

2 tablespoons minced fresh basil or 1 tablespoon dried basil

2 tablespoons minced fresh parsley

1 16-oz. can whole peeled tomatoes, drained

½ cup Sercial (dry) Madeira or ½ cup dry sherry

8 oz. tempeh

1 tablespoon olive oil

freshly grated Parmesan cheese

In a large, deep skillet, sauté the mushrooms in 1 tablespoon butter for 3 to 5 minutes. Stir in the garlic for 15 seconds, then add the herbs, drained tomatoes and wine. Break up the tomatoes with a knife or large spoon; bring the sauce to a boil and let simmer.

Brush the tempeh on both sides with olive oil. Broil 6 inches beneath the heating element until it is a rich golden brown, or about 5 minutes. Turn and brown other side; remove from oven.

About 5 minutes before you are ready to serve, slice the tempeh into bite-sized pieces and stir them into the sauce. If the sauce is too thin, stir 1 tablespoon arrowroot mixed with 2 tablespoons milk into the sauce to thicken it. If the sauce is of agreeable consistency but too acidic, stir in the milk only.

Spoon the Tempeh Scallopini over the spaghetti squash. Generously top with Parmesan cheese.

Cauliflower with Lemon and Green Onion

1 head of cauliflower

1 large green onion

½ tablespoon butter

1 tablespoon fresh lemon juice

Rinse and cut up the cauliflower into small flowerets. Finely slice the green onion, including a bit of the green. In a covered pot, melt the butter with 3 tablespoons water. Stir in the cauliflower and cover; cook until barely tender. (Check every 3 minutes to make sure your pot isn't dry and the cauliflower about to scorch.) Stir in the green onion, cover and cook 10 seconds longer. Toss with lemon juice; serve immediately.

Anthropologists estimate that ancient hunter-gatherers expended 1 calorie for every 10 calories of food they provided for themselves. These days, a beef farmer burns approximately 100 fossil fuel calories to provide us with 1 calorie of beef. Those who ask us to look at the global consequences of a meat-centered diet wield some powerful statistics. Frances Moore Lappé, in her tenth anniversary edition of Diet for a Small Planet, *points out that we exchange 16 pounds of grain and soybeans as cattle feed to provide ourselves with 1 pound of ground beef; if we ate the soybeans and grain instead, we'd receive 21 times more calories and 8 times more protein than we get from eating the pound of beef. Lappé also reports that "the water used to produce just 10 pounds of steak equals the household consumption of my family of three for an entire year."*

MEAT DISHES

Peasant's Cabbage Soup with Sausage

Swedish Cucumbers

Cornmeal Waffles with Savory Butter

SERVES 6 TO 8

TIME TO PREPARE

60 minutes

INGREDIENTS

ON HAND

- [ ] *2 quarts chicken stock*
- [ ] *3 eggs*
- [ ] *flour*
- [ ] *cornmeal*
- [ ] *baking powder*
- [ ] *baking soda*
- [ ] *butter*
- [ ] *vegetable oil*
- [ ] *white or cider vinegar (1 cup)*
- [ ] *sugar*
- [ ] *marjoram*
- [ ] *dill weed*
- [ ] *dry mustard*
- [ ] *Tabasco*

SHOPPING LIST

- [ ] *1 pint buttermilk*
- [ ] *½ lb. sweet butter*
- [ ] *3 oz. cheddar cheese*
- [ ] *¾ lb. kielbasa (Polish sausage)*
- [ ] *3 large carrots*
- [ ] *8 new potatoes (2 ½ cups diced)*
- [ ] *1 head of cabbage*
- [ ] *4 large leeks or 2 yellow onions*
- [ ] *celery*
- [ ] *3 large, firm cucumbers*
- [ ] *fresh chives*

This is a hearty meal for a crisp night. Serve it with a dark lager, eat by candlelight, forget the electric waffle iron in the background and you can imagine yourself a medieval peasant having your evening meal. Twelfth-century poets often mention waffles, which were made and sold on the streets. On the great religious feast days, the waffle-sellers baked their waffles in stalls which they set up next to the doors of the great cathedrals. The people ate the waffles piping hot; the best of them they called "métiers."

OVERVIEW

1. Begin the soup. As it simmers, prepare the cucumber salad. Chill the salad until you are ready to serve.

2. Prepare the waffles and savory butter.

Swedish Cucumbers

3 large, firm cucumbers

3 teaspoons salt

6 tablespoons sugar

1 cup white or cider vinegar

¾ tablespoon dill weed

Peel the cucumbers if the skin is bitter or heavily waxed. Slice very thin and sprinkle with the salt and sugar. Stir and let sit for a couple of minutes. Press the cucumbers with a large spoon to extrude their juice. Add the vinegar and dill weed. Stir well and refrigerate until serving. (Cucumbers dressed this way will keep for approximately two weeks in the refrigerator.)

Peasant's Cabbage Soup

1 tablespoon butter plus 1 tablespoon vegetable oil

2 cups finely chopped celery

2 cups finely chopped carrots

4 leeks cut in ½-inch pieces or 2 yellow onions, coarsely chopped

2 quarts chicken stock

2 cups sliced green cabbage

2 ½ cups potatoes, peeled and finely diced

½ teaspoon marjoram

1 teaspoon dill weed

¾ lb. kielbasa (Polish sausage), sliced thin

In a large heavy soup pot, sauté the celery, carrots and leeks or onion in the oil and butter. When the vegetables are softened, add the cabbage and cook 3 minutes. Add the stock and bring rapidly to a boil. Reduce the heat and simmer 15 minutes.

Add the potatoes and herbs. Simmer 15 minutes. Purée one-third of the soup in a blender or processor and return to the pot. Add the sliced sausage. Simmer 10 minutes. Season with salt and freshly ground pepper to taste.

Cornmeal Waffles with Savory Butter

WAFFLE BATTER

3 eggs

1 ½ cups buttermilk

⅓ cup melted sweet butter

¾ cup cornmeal

1 cup whole wheat or unbleached white flour

1 ½ tablespoons sugar

2 ½ teaspoons baking powder

1 teaspoon baking soda

½ teaspoon salt

⅓ cup grated cheddar cheese

SAVORY BUTTER

½ cup sweet butter, softened or cut into pats

1 teaspoon dry mustard

1 tablespoon or more fresh snipped chives

dash of Tabasco

Preheat the waffle iron. Put a large platter in a warm oven. Mix together the eggs, buttermilk and butter. In a separate bowl, stir together the dry ingredients and grated cheese. Add the dry ingredients to the liquid ingredients. Stir gently until the ingredients are combined.

Cook the waffles in the waffle iron according to the manufacturer's instructions. Cut the cooked waffles into pieces that can be handled like bread. Transfer to the warm platter in the oven, loosely covering them with foil so they don't dry out.

Blend together ingredients for savory butter in a processor or blender. Serve the waffles as you would warm bread; pass with savory butter.

Chinese Hot Pepper Beef and Asparagus

Bean Curd and Green Onions

Rice or Noodles

Chinese Hot Pepper Beef is one of those wonderful dishes you get at a Chinese restaurant and wish you knew how to make. Preparation of this basic dish is simple, and when fresh asparagus is out of season, you can use broccoli, zucchini or bell peppers in its place. Chinese Hot Pepper Beef satisfies one's appetite for beef in a 2- or 3-ounce serving and the recipe uses an economical and lean cut of meat.

SERVES 2

TIME TO PREPARE

30 minutes

INGREDIENTS

ON HAND

☐ *brown rice or noodles (any type)*
☐ *Chinese sesame oil*
☐ *vegetable oil*
☐ *soy sauce*
☐ *oyster sauce*
☐ *honey*
☐ *sugar*
☐ *fresh garlic*
☐ *Tabasco*
☐ *sesame seeds*
☐ *cornstarch*
☐ *chicken stock (½ cup, optional)*

SHOPPING LIST

☐ *6 oz. round steak or flank steak*
☐ *½ lb. firm tofu*
☐ *10 spears fresh asparagus (broccoli, zucchini, bell peppers or snow peas could be substituted)*
☐ *8 green onions*

OVERVIEW

1. If you precooked rice in the morning (*see page 99 for directions*) complete cooking the rice now. If you are starting rice from scratch, allow 45 minutes for it to cook. If you don't want to wait for rice to cook, substitute noodles or use converted rice.

2. Slice and marinate the steak.

3. You will have to stir-fry the beef dish and the tofu at the same time, so cut up all the vegetables and assemble all the ingredients before you begin.

4. Begin to sauté the tofu about 12 minutes before the rice is finished cooking. Or, if you are cooking noodles, begin to boil the water and then start to fry the tofu.

5. Prepare the beef dish.

6. As the sauce for the beef dish thickens, complete cooking the tofu dish.

Chinese Hot Pepper Beef

MARINADE

3 tablespoons soy sauce

1 clove garlic, pressed

1 tablespoon Chinese sesame oil

4 green onions (or substitute 1 leek)

1 tablespoon honey

½ teaspoon Tabasco

1 cup thinly sliced flank or round steak

½ cup chicken stock or water

10 spears fresh asparagus (broccoli, zucchini, bell pepper or snow peas could be substituted)

1 tablespoon cornstarch mixed with 2 tablespoons water

2 tablespoons toasted sesame seeds

It is easier to thinly slice partially frozen steak. Flank steak should be sliced on the diagonal and across the grain. One steak will last through a few Hot Pepper Beef suppers; wrap well the remaining steak and store in freezer.

Stir together the ingredients for the marinade. Marinate the sliced beef until you are ready to begin stir-frying. The longer the meat marinates, the more tender it will be.

Break off tough ends of asparagus and cut into 2-inch lengths. Slice the green onions or leeks. Prepare the cornstarch-water mixture. Drain the marinade into ½ cup chicken stock or water. Heat a skillet; quickly toast 2 tablespoons sesame seeds and set aside. In a dry, very hot skillet, stir-fry the beef 6 minutes, or until its color changes. Stir in the vegetables. Add the stock and stir until it comes to a boil. Cover and simmer until the vegetables are tender–crisp. Add the cornstarch mixture; stir until the sauce thickens. Garnish with toasted sesame seeds; serve immediately.

Bean Curd and Green Onions

vegetable oil

½ lb. firm tofu

4 green onions, cut into 1 ½-inch lengths, fresh stems included

½ teaspoon oyster sauce

½ teaspoon sugar

Slice the tofu horizontally into ½-inch slabs. Lay the tofu between several paper towels to absorb the moisture. Cut the tofu into 1-inch squares. In a nonstick or lightly oiled skillet, sauté the tofu so that it is golden brown on both sides. Add the green onions and oyster sauce. Stir and cover. Cook for one minute. Add the sugar and stir. The sugar will form a glaze. Serve hot.

Fennel-Spiced Italian Sausage and Broccoli with Pasta

Tomato and Red Onion Salad

Warm Crusty Bread

SERVES 4

(easily halved)

TIME TO PREPARE

30 minutes

INGREDIENTS

ON HAND
- ☐ *olive oil*
- ☐ *dry vermouth or dry white wine*
- ☐ *red wine vinegar*
- ☐ *fresh garlic*
- ☐ *fennel seeds*
- ☐ *basil*
- ☐ *Parmesan cheese*

SHOPPING LIST
- ☐ *8 oz. fettucine*
- ☐ *1 lb. Italian sausage (preferably bulk)*
- ☐ *1 small yellow onion*
- ☐ *1 red onion*
- ☐ *1 bunch broccoli*
- ☐ *2 red bell peppers (or green if red are unavailable)*
- ☐ *4 large ripe tomatoes*
- ☐ *2 oz. sunflower seeds or pine nuts*
- ☐ *1 loaf crusty bread*

It was in the hollow stalk of a fennel plant that Prometheus transported the fire which he had stolen from Mt. Olympus to give to mankind. Greek athletes in training ate fennel seeds to control their weight and Roman soldiers believed that eating fennel assured their strength and courage.

Traditionally, fennel seeds were boiled in wine and drunk as an antidote to serpent bites or poisonous herbs or mushrooms. Nursing mothers drank a brew of fennel seeds and barley water to increase their milk and make it more wholesome.

While there probably isn't enough fennel in this meal to produce any of these effects, it is interesting to note how fennel has been considered through the ages.

OVERVIEW

1. Turn the oven to 275°; wrap the bread in foil and begin to warm it.

2. Prepare the Tomato and Red Onion Salad. Cover and refrigerate.

3. Prepare the pasta dish. Serve.

Tomato and Red Onion Salad

4 large ripe tomatoes

1 red onion

2 cloves garlic, minced

1 tablespoon red wine vinegar

2 teaspoons minced fresh basil
or 1 teaspoon dried basil

2 teaspoons olive oil

salt and freshly ground pepper to
taste

Slice the tomatoes into ½ inch-thick slices. Slice the onion paper thin. Put one layer of tomato slices in a serving bowl. Sprinkle with some of the basil, olive oil, vinegar, garlic, salt and freshly ground black pepper. Cover with slices of onion; sprinkle with more olive oil, vinegar and seasonings, then add another layer of tomato slices. Continue to layer the ingredients in this way. Chill until serving.

Fennel-Spiced Italian Sausage and Broccoli with Pasta

1 bunch broccoli

1 tablespoon olive oil

1 lb. Italian sausage (preferably
bulk)

1 small yellow onion, chopped

4 large cloves garlic, minced or
pressed

2 red bell peppers cut into ¼-inch
strips (use green if red aren't
available)

2 oz. sunflower seeds or pine nuts
(2 tablespoons)

4 teaspoons fennel seeds

2 tablespoons dry vermouth (dry
white wine is a less flavorful but
possible substitute)

8 oz. fettucine

freshly grated Parmesan cheese to
pass at the table

Prepare the broccoli: cut off and divide flowerets; peel the tough outer skin from the stem and cut into bite-sized pieces. In a pot large enough to boil the water for the pasta, steam the broccoli until tender-crisp. Rinse under cold water and drain. Start to boil water to cook the pasta.

Remove casings from sausages, if necessary. Heat 1 tablespoon olive oil in a heavy skillet. Over medium high heat, sauté the sausage, breaking it up into small bits. When it is golden, stir in the onion and garlic. When the onion is soft, stir in the broccoli, pepper, sunflower seeds or pine nuts, fennel seeds and vermouth. Reduce the heat to medium and cover. (The pasta should be nearly done by this point.) Sauté only until the broccoli is heated thoroughly.

When the fettucine is cooked *al dente*, drain and rinse under hot water. Drain well. Add to the vegetables and sausage. Toss. Serve immediately on warm plates.

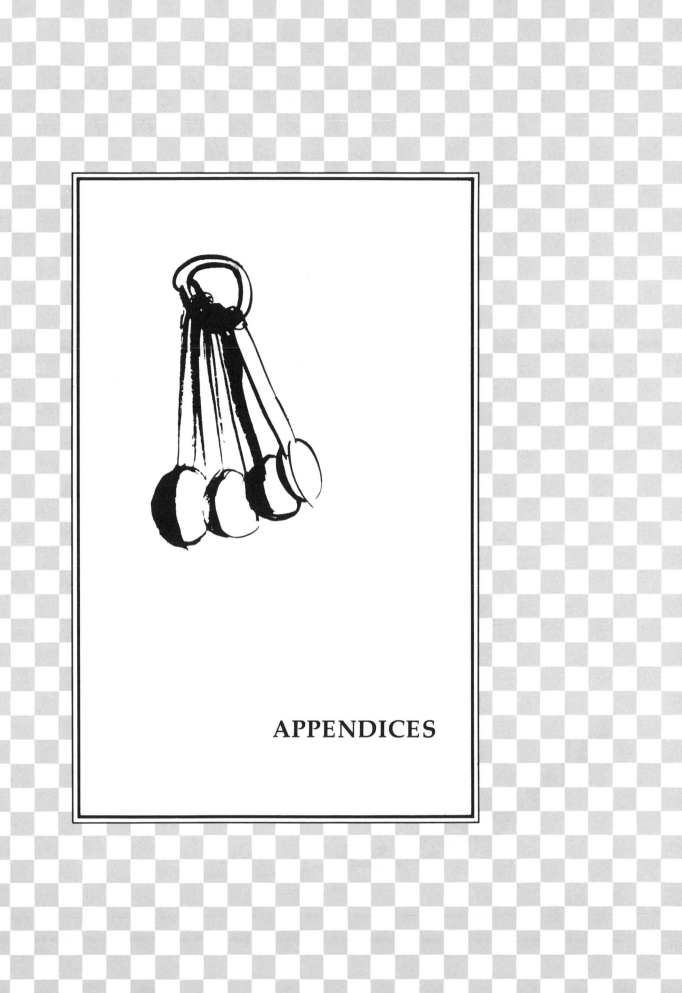

APPENDICES

APPENDIX I

Techniques of Quick Cooking or Don't Start Every Meal from Scratch

It is estimated that ancient food gatherers spent a third of their waking hours in search of food. Until the Industrial Revolution 220 years ago, hunting, gathering, cultivating and preserving food were *primary* occupations for 90% of the world's population. Today, the average person spends a third of his or her income to purchase food—and we still have to spend time preparing food.

A brief thumbing through traditional cookbooks makes it abundantly clear, however, that efficiency did not shape our methods of food preparation. Traditionally, Mother, Grandmother or cook was in the kitchen several hours a day, a kitchen which did not contain a freezer, food processor or microwave oven. Few people lived in "individual households," and mothers and fathers weren't taking exercise classes, going to their children's soccer games, working for eight hours, commuting and cooking dinner, too.

Demands on our time have certainly changed, and these changes call for more than some "quick fix" recipes. We need a systematic revamping of our approach to cooking so that we can more quickly prepare classic dishes—dishes that use fresh, nutritious ingredients and that are pleasing to the eye and palate, as well.

This chapter contains many ideas to streamline the preparation of meals. The suggestions involve organization, preplanning, and the preparation of foodstuffs in large batches to reduce single, repetitive efforts. Once initiated, you'll find these small changes provide a sense of ease.

Organize and Stock Your Freezer Like Another Cupboard

On a quiet evening or rainy Saturday afternoon, as you listen to a special radio program, or whenever you have the urge to immerse yourself in the textures and smells of food, prepare some of the following components of meals ahead of time.

ONIONS —can be chopped in quantity and frozen. Flash freeze by spreading the chopped onion on a cookie sheet; place uncovered in the freezer. When frozen, store in a heavy or doubled plastic bag. One onion equals about ¾ cup chopped. This is an especially easy operation if you have a food processor. It can also maximize your food budget if you buy the onions on sale or in bulk at a farmer's market.

GARLIC —can be minced by hand or in the food processor and frozen. One clove of garlic equals about ½ teaspoon minced.

PARMESAN CHEESE —can be grated in quantity and kept in the freezer. It remains "freshly grated."

PARSLEY —can be chopped when it begins to look tired and then put into the freezer. Use in recipes as fresh parsley.

TOMATO PASTE —can be frozen in individual 1-tablespoon portions in sandwich-sized plastic bags (several tablespoons to a bag frozen flat). Use the tomato paste while still frozen. If a recipe calls for only 2 or 3 tablespoons, you won't have to open a whole can and risk spoiling the unused portion.

CREPES —freeze well and provide the basis for an elegant, simple meal. Layer them between waxed paper, slide into a plastic bag, and freeze flat. Remove as many crepes as you want for a meal. Prepare a filling, then stuff and bake the crepes. If you are stuffing only a few crepes, save energy by heating them on top of the stove in a covered, heavy iron skillet.

CHICKEN BREASTS —can be boned, pounded and layered between waxed paper, then frozen. These can be sautéed while still frozen and used as the basis for many quick, delicious suppers.

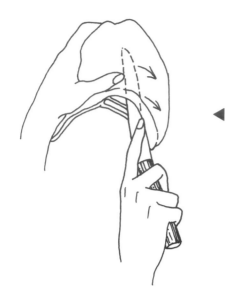

Boning a chicken breast is a technique that takes only two or three minutes and can be easily mastered with just a little practice. The greatest asset is a very sharp boning knife. You can bone a whole or halved breast.

To bone a chicken breast, place the breast skin–side up with the ribs towards you. Insert the tip of the knife between the rib cage and the flesh. Work the knife flat and as close as possible along the ribs towards the other end, thus separating the meat from the ribs. The flesh will still be attached to the center bone.

Repeat this process on the other side if you are boning a whole breast. Now use the tip of the knife to cut the meat away from wishbone. Lift the fillet, scraping the meat away from the rib cage towards the center bone. Move the knife along the center bone, carefully separating the flesh from the bone without tearing the meat.

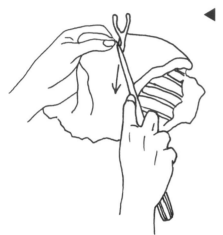

Lift the fillet away from the breast bone. Cut away the skin and fat. Flip the breast over and remove the silvery tendons; pull at the tendon with one hand while delicately cutting it free from the flesh with the other. Cut the whole breast in half.

Pound the boned chicken breast before freezing. Place the meat between two sheets of waxed paper, tucking the small extending tip under the larger portion. Gently pound with a rolling pin or the flat side of a cleaver until the breast is a uniform ¼ inch thick.

For Oriental dishes, do not pound the boned chicken breast; rather, cut it into strips and across into bite-sized pieces before freezing.

CHICKEN STOCK

- [ ] 5 lbs. chicken parts (Backs, necks, wing tips, breast bones, etc. not used in preparing a chicken meal can be collected in a large plastic bag in the freezer to make stock.)
- [ ] 2 carrots
- [ ] 1 stalk of celery, with leaves
- [ ] 1 bay leaf
- [ ] ¼ teaspoon thyme or a few fresh sprigs
- [ ] 8 to 10 peppercorns
- [ ] 2 teaspoons salt
- [ ] 5 quarts water

—on hand makes all kinds of delicious meals possible. It will keep for 7 days in the refrigerator and 6 months in the freezer. Here is a basic recipe that makes 3 quarts of stock:

Put the ingredients into a large pot. Bring to a boil; reduce heat. Simmer uncovered for 3 hours. Skim the scum that rises to the surface. Remove the vegetables and chicken to a refrigerator bowl.

Strain the stock through a fine mesh strainer or cheese cloth. Refrigerate or freeze. Skim off the fat that rises to the surface before using. If you are going to freeze the stock, skim off the fat first so that you can use it straight from the freezer. Do not freeze in ordinary glass jars; they can crack. The cheapest and handiest freezer containers are well-rinsed milk cartons. Pour in the cooled, defatted stock and staple the carton closed. You can tear away the container and put the frozen stock directly into a pot to heat.

LEGUMES —such as dried beans, peas and lentils can be prepared in large batches and frozen in different sized containers for a variety of uses. Beans pop out of plastic containers and can be brought to serving temperature in about 10 minutes. Add them to vegetable soup, or purée and season them for a quick bean soup, or sauté and mash them with onions for frijoles refritos. Dal, an easy–to–prepare spicy Indian dish made with lentils, mung beans or split peas, is nice to keep on hand in the freezer; use to complement curried dishes or a simple meal of rice and steamed vegetables. (*See page 69 for a recipe for dal.*)

Having cooked legumes in the freezer will encourage you to incorporate this thrifty, low-fat source of protein into your diet. Legumes are also an excellent source of fiber which has been found to reduce the blood's cholesterol and stabilize the blood's sugar level.

SAUCES —are usually as easy to cook in large quantity as for one meal. Freeze extra sauce in plastic containers or milk or yogurt containers. The sauce will pop out of a plastic container; the milk or yogurt container can be torn away. The sauce can then be warmed while still frozen.

Label the sauce—what it is, when it was made, and how much is in the container. As a rule of thumb, 1 cup of tomato sauce tops 2 servings of pasta; ¾ cup of pesto will sauce 1 pound of pasta which is 4 dinner-sized servings. (*See pages 105–109 for a variety of sauce recipes.*)

THE RUNNING INVENTORY

This is the key to using a freezer effectively. Otherwise, frozen food becomes something stored rather than utilized. Just begin. Get a small file box, index cards, gummed labels and a pen. Pull everything out of the freezer and write out an individual card for each thing: what it is; how much of it you have; and, when it was frozen. Before putting the food back into the freezer, clearly label each container. Small gummed labels work fine.

Set up sections in your file box for meats, soups, sauces, legumes, etc. and file the cards under the appropriate categories. Now when you are tired, rushed, low on fresh supplies or don't know what to make, check your inventory to see what's in the freezer. You will also be able to see how long food has been in the freezer and what should be eaten. Keep the file box, extra index cards, gummed labels and a pen near the freezer. Once you get started, you'll be surprised how easy it is to keep this system up. Every time you use something from the freezer cross it off the appropriate index card and your inventory will always be up to date.

Organizing the Kitchen

KEEPING BASIC STAPLES ON HAND

These are the basic staples I keep on hand. With them I can always put together something fairly interesting to eat; all I need to add are fresh vegetables and tofu, fish or poultry. The herbs and spice list, which is lengthy, allows me to prepare basic dishes from a fairly wide range of cuisines including Mexican, Italian, French, Indian and Chinese.

OILS
- [ ] *olive oil*
- [ ] *a light oil such as corn, safflower, or sunflower seed*
- [ ] *Chinese sesame oil*

VINEGARS
- [ ] *red wine vinegar*
- [ ] *white wine vinegar*
- [ ] *white vinegar*
- [ ] *rice vinegar*

WINES
- [ ] *dry sherry*
- [ ] *dry vermouth (to use when I don't have an opened bottle of dry white wine in the refrigerator)*

DRY GOODS
- [ ] *whole wheat flour*
- [ ] *cornmeal*
- [ ] *baking powder*
- [ ] *baking soda*
- [ ] *arrowroot or cornstarch*
- [ ] *sugar*
- [ ] *brown rice*
- [ ] *cracked wheat*
- [ ] *lentils*
- [ ] *fettucine noodles*
- [ ] *sesame seeds (brown unhulled)*
- [ ] *pine nuts or sunflower seeds*

DAIRY
- [ ] *butter*
- [ ] *nonfat milk*
- [ ] *Parmesan cheese (freshly grated and stored in freezer)*

HERBS AND SPICES
- [ ] *salt*
- [ ] *whole black peppercorns*
- [ ] *cayenne*
- [ ] *Tabasco*
- [ ] *paprika*
- [ ] *chili powder*
- [ ] *dried red pepper flakes*
- [ ] *fresh garlic*
- [ ] *fresh and powdered ginger*
- [ ] *powdered mustard*
- [ ] *turmeric*
- [ ] *curry powder*
- [ ] *ground cumin*
- [ ] *cumin seeds*
- [ ] *ground coriander*
- [ ] *basil*
- [ ] *oregano*
- [ ] *marjoram*
- [ ] *thyme*
- [ ] *tarragon*
- [ ] *dill weed*
- [ ] *fennel seeds*
- [ ] *cinnamon*
- [ ] *nutmeg*

CANNED GOODS
- [ ] *tomato sauce*
- [ ] *whole peeled tomatoes*
- [ ] *tomato paste*
- [ ] *black olives*
- [ ] *green olives*
- [ ] *garbanzo beans*
- [ ] *kidney beans*
- [ ] *tuna packed in water*

PRODUCE
- [ ] *yellow onions*
- [ ] *carrots*
- [ ] *celery*
- [ ] *fresh parsley*
- [ ] *lemons*
- [ ] *small red potatoes*

MISCELLANEOUS
- [ ] *vegetable bouillon cubes or powder*
- [ ] *Dijon-type mustard*
- [ ] *soy sauce*
- [ ] *oyster sauce*
- [ ] *capers*
- [ ] *honey*
- [ ] *molasses**
- [ ] *vanilla extract*
- [ ] *raisins*
- [ ] *chicken stock (frozen homecooked)*
- [ ] *refried beans (either canned or frozen)*
- [ ] *corn tortillas (frozen)*
- [ ] *eggs*

*Brown sugar can be made by adding molasses back to granulated sugar, just like the sugar companies do; 1 tablespoon molasses added to ½ cup of sugar will make ½ cup brown sugar. Measure the sugar and then the molasses into a food processor or blender and whirl together. This is much cheaper than buying brown sugar and with molasses on hand you can bake gingerbread and bran muffins.

The way I keep these items in stock is simple; when I run out of something, I write it down on a piece of paper stuck under a magnet (in the shape of the Mad Hatter) on the refrigerator. This is the start of my next shopping list.

Many health food stores sell herbs and spices in bulk; the advantage to buying them this way is they cost considerably less. The key to determining the freshness, and therefore pungency, of herbs and spices is smell (crush dried green herbs between your fingers) and the brightness of color.

KNOWING WHERE YOUR TOOLS ARE

I have all kinds of things crammed into my kitchen cupboards and drawers: old calendars I'm saving to wrap gifts; my grandmother's baking pans which I never use but can't throw out; jars in case I do some canning one day, etc. I realized that I do nearly all my cooking with about 20% of the objects stored in the kitchen, so I separated out this 20% and put it into certain drawers and on particular shelves. Now I know exactly where the big soup pot (and its lid) is, the garlic press, the steaming trivet. . . . Such a simple, happy change!

Measuring cups that double as scoopers save a surprising amount of time. The awkward step of spooning flour from a crock into a measuring cup is forever eliminated. "Scoopers" come as a set of ¼, ⅓, ½, and 1 cup scoops. Hang them, and your measuring spoons, in a handy location so that you won't have to dig them out of a drawer each time you need them. Likewise, keep your herbs, baking soda and powder, and other staple cooking ingredients in handy locations that don't change. You will be amazed at the ease this small amount of organization provides.

Using a Crockpot

The electric slow cooker, or Crockpot, is a little like a surrogate mother. It spends all day cooking nurturing stews, thick soups, long-simmering sauces (things you would never have time to prepare when you're at work all day), and has them ready for you when you get home tired and hungry. Crockpot cooking reverses your schedule. You put together the main course in the morning; the food cooks all day and is done in the evening. All that's left to do is fix a salad and warm some bread.

You can also bake apples and potatoes. Just wrap them individually in foil and stack them inside the pot. Cover and cook on a low setting for approximately 6 hours. On a low setting, most slow cookers use less electricity than a 100 watt light bulb, so they are more energy efficient to use than your oven.

Using a Crockpot can be a convenient way to prepare large batches of basics—sauces, chicken stock, or beans, for example, to stock your freezer. If you are cooking for yourself and/or only one other person, your cooking time becomes twice as efficient. Just freeze half the pot of stew or soup that you make.

Crockpots have other advantages, too. Vitamins and minerals are retained that can be lost or destroyed in other methods of cooking. The lid forms an airtight seal so nutrients aren't lost in escaping steam. The nutrient-rich cooking broth becomes part of the meal rather than tossed down the drain as in steaming. Vitamin A, which is destroyed in high temperature stir-frying, remains stable in Crockpot cooking.

Another advantage to using a slow cooker is that food is cooked at such a low temperature on the low setting, it doesn't matter if it cooks longer than is called for in a recipe. I have made wonderful 24-hour chili. One warning, however. Do not indiscriminately remove the lid from the cooker when you are cooking on "low." It takes a long time for the unit to regain its cooking heat.

Quick Cooking Rice and Legumes

A few moments spent precooking brown rice, lentils, and split peas in the morning will save you a great deal of time in the evening. From scratch, they take about 45 minutes to cook, but precooked they can be ready to serve in 10 to 30 minutes, depending on the technique used.

"INSTANT" BROWN RICE

—in the morning, bring to boil in a covered pot a measure of rice and twice that amount of water. Boil for 10 minutes. Turn off the heat and let sit several hours, or all day. In the evening, the rice is cooked perfectly and need only be reheated.

TEN-MINUTE BROWN RICE

—in the morning, bring to boil in a covered pot a measure of rice and twice that amount of water. Turn off heat and let sit several hours or all day. In the evening, the rice will be perfectly cooked in 10 minutes.

THIRTY-MINUTE BROWN RICE

—soak the rice all day in its cooking water. That evening, bring the water and rice to a boil, cover and cook over low heat until craters form on the surface.

TEN-MINUTE LENTILS, SPLIT PEAS AND MUNG BEANS

—in the morning, bring the legumes to a boil in their cooking water. Turn off the heat and keep the pot covered. In the evening, bring the legumes to a second boil, season, and simmer until soft, or about 10 minutes.

Without precooking, lentils will take 30 to 45 minutes to prepare. Red lentils, however, are special; this variety cooks, from start to finish, in about 10 minutes. If you are fond of lentil dishes, track down a source for the red or brilliant orange variety; they can often be found in health food stores.

Why make the effort to use brown rice? White rice contains only 33% of the niacin, less than 50% of the B6, 20% of the thiamin, and 60% of the riboflavin in brown rice. If you *must* use white rice, "converted" or parboiled rice is preferable; parboiling forces some of the vitamins from the husk into the endosperm—the "white rice" grains. "Instant" and "minute" rice have the least nutritional value. Long and short brown rice have nearly equivalent nutritional value.

APPENDIX II

Tossed Greens and Vinaigrette Dressings

Although you will find listed in this cookbook "Tossed Greens with Vinaigrette Dressing" as a course in several menus, this is not meant to suggest eating the same thing night after night. The salad is an open field, so to speak, for experimentation and creativity.

You could, for example, use just one type of lettuce (butter lettuce is very nice on its own), or mix several types of greens. You might like to include the hot, peppery leaves of watercress, young mustard greens, or rocket (also called roquette, rugula or arugula)*. In the winter you might gravitate towards the chewy, pungent leaves of young beet greens or chard. Napa (or Chinese) cabbage has little taste but provides a light crisp texture. A grated raw beet, thinly sliced red cabbage or strips of red pepper add visual interest.

Tossed greens can be varied by the addition of fresh or dried herbs, spices, cheese, nuts, and seeds. Dill weed, coriander, mint, basil, oregano, thyme, tarragon, celery seeds, toasted sesame seeds, tamari roasted sunflower seeds, fresh minced garlic, and anise are just a few of the possibilities. Combining herbs and spices is a subtle art; fennel and mint, for example, are unexpectedly delightful together. Or whisk a small amount of ground spices into the portion of the vinaigrette you'll be using for the evening's salad: a pinch of curry, smokey paprika, a bit of cayenne, ground cumin and coriander, or ginger and soy sauce give a fresh personality to a simple salad. A warning, however: use a light hand in trying out herbs and spices; they can easily and unpleasantly dominate the delicate balance of a salad.

There also exists a world of exotic oils and vinegars for you to experiment with in preparing salad dressings—walnut oil, esoteric brands of extra virgin (or first pressed) olive oil, Balsamic vinegar, sherry vinegar, raspberry vinegar and so on. There really is endless room for experimentation, so don't imagine only one corollary to "Tossed Greens with Vinaigrette." Imagine instead, and then create, a salad that will perfectly complement your meal's tastes, colors and textures.

*Seeds for rocket are available through Northrup King and Burpee. Calling rocket "hardy" is an understatement; I have been brutally careless in my handling of the seedlings and yet they grow on. Pinch the flower buds as they form and the plants will continue to send out leaves, but if you allow a few plants to go to seed, you will have many healthy volunteers.

Salad Dressings

The simplest and most delicious salad dressing is made of freshly squeezed lemon juice, minced garlic and the best tasting extra virgin olive oil you can find. The ratio I enjoy is:

1 *small clove garlic*

3 *tablespoons lemon juice*

3 *tablespoons olive oil*

Prepare the dressing when you begin making dinner so that the garlic has time to flavor the oil and lemon juice. Strain the dressing onto the greens just before serving.

It is also convenient to have dressing on hand. If you buy bottled dressing, please note that:

1. you *can* make a good-tasting dressing (in fact, it will taste better than the bottled type);

2. it is cheaper to blend your own dressing than to buy it prepackaged;

3. you will avoid ingesting the preservatives and additives many bottled and packaged dressings contain; and,

4. by using polyunsaturated oils (corn, safflower, soy or sunflower, for example), you will avoid the saturated oils in bottled dressings that can raise your blood cholesterol level.

Here are recipes for basic vinaigrette, vinaigrette variations and other dressings which you can keep on hand in your refrigerator. Olive oil solidifies in the refrigerator, so you'll need to take an olive oil dressing out of the refrigerator when you begin to prepare a meal, to give the oil time to liquify.

The last four salad dressings given are made with little or no oil; they are useful when you want to reduce your intake of oils and fats, or to dress a salad that includes high-fat ingredients such as avocado, nuts and cheese.

Basic Vinaigrette

☐ *¾ cup oil (preferably 3 tablespoons light-flavored olive oil plus safflower oil)*

☐ *¼ cup red wine vinegar*

☐ *1 teaspoon salt*

☐ *freshly ground pepper to taste*

Put all the ingredients into a jar with a tight-fitting lid. Shake well. Store in the refrigerator.

A Sharper Vinaigrette

- ☐ ½ cup oil
- ☐ ½ teaspoon dried or 1 teaspoon fresh oregano
- ☐ ¼ cup red wine vinegar
- ☐ ¼ teaspoon salt
- ☐ ⅛ teaspoon freshly ground black pepper
- ☐ 1 teaspoon Dijon-type mustard

Put all the ingredients into a jar with a tight-fitting lid. Shake well. Store in the refrigerator.

Shallot-Tarragon Vinaigrette

- ☐ 1 cup oil (¼ cup olive oil plus ¾ cup safflower oil)
- ☐ ½ cup white wine vinegar
- ☐ 2 tablespoons fresh or 3 teaspoons dried tarragon
- ☐ 1 tablespoon Dijon-type mustard
- ☐ 3 shallots, finely minced
- ☐ salt and freshly ground pepper to taste

Put all the ingredients into a jar with a tight-fitting lid. Shake well. Store in the refrigerator.

Parsley Vinaigrette

- ☐ ¼ cup chopped fresh parsley
- ☐ ½ teaspoon salt
- ☐ ¾ cup oil (3 tablespoons light-flavored olive oil plus safflower oil)
- ☐ ¼ cup red wine vinegar
- ☐ 1 shallot, finely minced
- ☐ freshly ground pepper to taste

Put all the ingredients into a jar with a tight-fitting lid. Shake well. Store in the refrigerator.

Vinaigrette with Salad Herbs

- ☐ 2 tablespoons Salad Herbs
- ☐ ⅔ cup oil (3 tablespoons light-flavored olive oil plus safflower oil)
- ☐ ⅓ cup red wine vinegar or lemon juice
- ☐ salt and freshly ground pepper to taste

Here is an excellent herb mixture to keep on hand. Combine 2 tablespoons of each of the following herbs in a jar: dried chervil; dried basil; celery seed; dried parsley; dried dill weed; and dried marjoram. Label "Salad Herbs," and use as described below.

Put all ingredients into a jar with a tight-fitting lid. Shake well and use.

Sherry Dressing

- ☐ ¼ cup light-flavored olive oil
- ☐ ⅓ cup dry sherry
- ☐ 3 tablespoons white vinegar
- ☐ 1 teaspoon lime juice
- ☐ ¼ teaspoon salt
- ☐ a pinch of curry powder

Put all the ingredients into a jar with a tight-fitting lid. Shake well. Store in the refrigerator. This light dressing is especially good on butter lettuce or spinach salads.

Miso-Ginger Dressing

- ☐ ¾ cup oil
- ☐ 4 tablespoons lemon juice or rice vinegar
- ☐ 4 tablespoons red miso or Hatcho miso (see page 105)
- ☐ ½ teaspoon Chinese sesame oil
- ☐ ⅛ teaspoon powdered mustard
- ☐ ¼ to ½ teaspoon grated fresh ginger
- ☐ 1 clove garlic, pressed

Combine ingredients in a blender or food processor. Store in refrigerator.

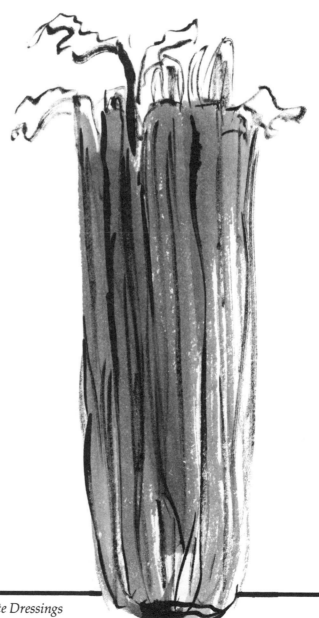

French Dressing

- ☐ 1 tablespoon oil
- ☐ ½ cup cider vinegar
- ☐ 1 tablespoon honey
- ☐ ½ teaspoon basil or ¼ teaspoon tarragon
- ☐ ½ teaspoon oregano
- ☐ 1 teaspoon chopped chives
- ☐ salt to taste

Put all the ingredients into a jar with a tight-fitting lid. Shake well. Store in the refrigerator.

Tomato Dressing

- ☐ the juice of ½ lemon
- ☐ 2 teaspoons apple cider vinegar
- ☐ 1 large, ripe tomato
- ☐ ½ teaspoon celery seeds
- ☐ ⅛ teaspoon basil
- ☐ ⅛ teaspoon tarragon
- ☐ ⅛ teaspoon oregano
- ☐ ⅛ teaspoon salt

Put all the ingredients into a blender or food processor. Blend together. Store in the refrigerator. Makes about 1 cup.

Italian Dressing

- ☐ ½ teaspoon oregano
- ☐ ½ teaspoon powdered mustard
- ☐ ½ teaspoon paprika
- ☐ ⅛ teaspoon thyme
- ☐ ⅛ teaspoon rosemary
- ☐ ¼ cup cider vinegar
- ☐ ¼ cup fresh lemon juice
- ☐ 1 clove garlic, mashed

Blend all the ingredients together. Let the dressing sit for 2 days in the refrigerator before using.

Roquefort Dressing

- ☐ 1 cup low-fat cottage cheese
- ☐ ½ cup buttermilk
- ☐ 3 tablespoons white or cider vinegar
- ☐ 3 oz. Roquefort or bleu cheese
- ☐ salt and freshly ground black pepper to taste

If you like a smooth dressing, combine all the ingredients in a blender or food processor and process until creamy. If you prefer a chunky dressing, only blend in half the cheese. After processing, crumble and stir in the remaining cheese.

APPENDIX III

Quick to Prepare Sauces

A good tasting sauce can harmonize the odds and ends you find in the refrigerator and cupboards into a lovely, simple meal. A sauce enlivens and makes special what otherwise would be rather ordinary fare.

Sauces can also be the key to solving the "what to serve the vegetarian coming for dinner?" problem. Attractively arrange steamed or sautéed vegetables and perhaps some tofu on noodles or grains, top with Miso Mushroom Sauce, Tahini Sauce, or Cheese Sauce with a Snap, prepare a salad, and you have a lovely, easy "vegetarian" meal.

Following are a variety of sauces, some traditional and some rather unusual. All are quick to prepare, and fats and oils are used as meagerly as possible without compromising the flavor or texture of the sauce.

*Miso Mushroom Sauce—**

—*gives a spicy heartiness to grains and vegetables.*

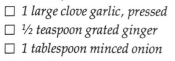

- ☐ 1 tablespoon butter
- ☐ 1 large clove garlic, pressed
- ☐ ½ teaspoon grated ginger
- ☐ 1 tablespoon minced onion
- ☐ 5 fresh mushrooms, washed and thinly sliced
- ☐ ⅓ cup tomato paste
- ☐ 1 tablespoon Hatcho miso or red miso*
- ☐ black pepper to taste

Melt the butter in a small skillet over medium heat. Stir in the garlic, ginger and onion. Sauté until the onion is soft. Stir in the mushrooms and cover. Cook for 2 minutes or until the mushrooms are tender. Reduce the heat to medium low. Add the tomato paste and miso; stir until smooth. Add water, a tablespoon at a time, until you achieve desired consistency. Stir after each addition of water. About 4 tablespoons should do it. Cover and cook 1 minute. Season with pepper to taste. Enough for 2 servings.

*Miso can be found either packaged or in bulk at health food stores and Asian groceries that carry Japanese foods. Used in the preparation of sauces and soups, miso is made from fermented soybeans or other grains. There are several types of miso; I recommend *Hatcho* miso, made from soybeans that have been aged for 2 years, or red miso which is also made from soybeans but not aged as long. Either would be appropriate to use in most recipes.

Miso stored in the refrigerator will keep for months, perhaps years. One tablespoon mixed with a cup of boiling water makes a pleasantly salty, low-fat and energizing broth to drink on a cold winter's day. Mix the boiling water in a little bit at a time to stir the miso smooth.

Cheese Sauce with a Snap—

—for steamed vegetables and grains, noodles, or steamed potatoes, or over stuffed crepes and omelettes.

- ☐ 2 tablespoons butter
- ☐ 2 minced shallots
- ☐ 2 tablespoons flour
- ☐ 1 cup milk
- ☐ ½ cup grated cheese (Farmer's, Jack, Swiss, or cheddar)
- ☐ ¼ teaspoon powdered mustard
- ☐ 1 tablespoon dry sherry or white wine
- ☐ a few drops Tabasco
- ☐ salt to taste

Melt the butter in a saucepan. Sauté the shallots until soft. Stir in the flour and brown it. Add the milk a small amount at a time, stirring until smooth each time before adding more. Continue cooking until the sauce thickens, stirring constantly. When the sauce has thickened, add the remaining ingredients. Stir thoroughly. Adjust seasonings. Serve hot.

This sauce can be stored for a week in the refrigerator.

Chili Tomato Sauce—

—an enchilada sauce, for huevos rancheros, or Spanish rice.

- ☐ 1 tablespoon white or apple cider vinegar
- ☐ 1 ½ teaspoons chili powder
- ☐ ½ teaspoon ground cumin
- ☐ ½ teaspoon ground coriander
- ☐ 1 15-oz. can tomato purée
- ☐ salt and Tabasco to taste

Combine ingredients in a saucepan and heat.

This sauce can be frozen or kept for a week in the refrigerator.

Pesto—

- ☐ 4 tablespoons soft butter
- ☐ 4 tablespoons walnuts
- ☐ 4 tablespoons sunflower seeds or pine nuts
- ☐ ½ cup olive oil
- ☐ 1 cup parsley leaves, loosely packed
- ☐ 3 cups fresh basil leaves, packed
- ☐ ¾ cup freshly grated Parmesan cheese
- ☐ 2 or more cloves garlic, pressed
- ☐ salt to taste

—could make shredded cardboard seem inviting. Not only is it wonderful on pasta, but pesto is delicious tossed with steamed new potatoes or stirred into soups, omelettes, crepe stuffings, or casseroles. Three-fourths cup of pesto will sauce 1 pound of pasta, which will feed four people. This recipe makes 1 ½ cups.

Melt 1 tablespoon butter in a heavy skillet. Stir in the walnuts and sunflower seeds or pine nuts; toast them for a couple of minutes. Place in a blender or food processor. Chop fine. Put half the olive oil into the blender, then the parsley and basil leaves. Turn on the machine and slowly add the rest of the oil. Add the Parmesan, remaining butter and pressed garlic. Blend until the ingredients form a thick paste.

Fresh basil is available in summer only, but pesto freezes well. A convenient method of storing pesto is to first freeze it in ice cube trays, then transfer the cubes to a heavy plastic bag. You can throw a cube into a pot of soup, or quickly warm several cubes to sauce a pasta dish.

You can also keep pesto in a jar in the refrigerator for several months, but you must keep a seal of olive oil over the top surface. Each time you spoon out some pesto, add more olive oil to keep a ¼- inch olive oil "cap."

Winter Pesto—

- ☐ 3 cups fresh spinach leaves, stems removed (frozen spinach will not do)
- ☐ 2 tablespoons soft butter
- ☐ 2 tablespoons walnuts
- ☐ 2 tablespoons sunflower seeds or pine nuts
- ☐ ½ cup olive oil
- ☐ 1 ½ cups fresh parsley
- ☐ 1 ½ teaspoons dried basil
- ☐ 4 cloves garlic, pressed
- ☐ 4 tablespoons freshly grated Parmesan cheese and 4 tablespoons freshly grated Romano cheese (or use all Parmesan)

—is a discovery for pesto lovers who run out of fresh basil pesto during the winter. I find it just as tasty.

Wash, dry and coarsely chop the spinach. Melt 1 tablespoon butter in a heavy skillet; toast the walnuts and sunflower seeds or pine nuts a couple of minutes. Put into a blender or food processor and chop. Pour ½ cup olive oil into the blender, and then add 1 cup spinach leaves. Blend smooth. Continue adding the spinach 1 cup at a time, blending the mixture smooth each time. Add the remaining ingredients and blend into a thick paste.

Tahini Sauce*—

—gives a rich garlicky flavor to grains, vegetables and fish.

- ☐ 4 tablespoons tahini (sesame butter)
- ☐ 4 tablespoons plain yogurt or buttermilk
- ☐ 1 teaspoon fresh lemon juice
- ☐ 2 tablespoons minced parsley
- ☐ 1 green onion, including fresh stem, sliced
- ☐ 1 small clove garlic, pressed
- ☐ dash of cayenne
- ☐ ⅛ teaspoon soy sauce
- ☐ ¼ teaspoon ground cumin
- ☐ salt or more soy sauce to taste

Combine all the ingredients in a food processor or blender. Serve at room temperature. (This sauce will keep for 2 weeks in the refrigerator.)

*Tahini, which is made of ground sesame seeds, is similar to a nut butter, and is used in Middle Eastern cuisine to make sauces, spreads, soups and cookies. Tahini can be found in jars or tins or in bulk at health food stores, gourmet shops or grocery stores that carry Middle Eastern foods.

Tahini can be made from raw or toasted sesame seeds; the toasted version is tastier. Tahini is a rich source of calcium and a tasty alternative to butter on your morning toast; try it spread with a bit of honey.

Basic Chinese Stir-Fry Sauce—

—is an excellent marinade for fish, chicken or tofu. It can be used in baking, barbecuing or stir-frying.

- ☐ 2 teaspoons vinegar (apple cider, malt or dark vinegar)
- ☐ 1 tablespoon sake or dry sherry
- ☐ 1 clove garlic, pressed
- ☐ 1 tablespoon grated ginger
- ☐ 2 teaspoons Chinese sesame oil
- ☐ ½ cup water or chicken stock
- ☐ ½ cup soy sauce
- ☐ ½ cup minced green onions, including stems
- ☐ 2 teaspoons sugar or honey
- ☐ Tabasco (optional)

FOR STIR-FRYING

Prepare the marinade. Mix 4 tablespoons of the marinade with 2 tablespoons cornstarch and set aside. Cut the tofu, fish, chicken or meat into bite-sized pieces and stir into the marinade. Cut up the vegetables.

Drain and reserve the marinade; stir-fry the tofu, fish, chicken or meat in a bit of oil. Remove from skillet and set aside. Stir-fry the vegetables in a bit of water or oil over medium high heat. If you are cooking a combination of vegetables, begin with the slowest cooking vegetable; cover the skillet or wok between stirrings. Use your judgment as to when each type of vegetable should be added; you want them all tender–crisp at the same time.

Stir smooth the cornstarch-marinade mixture and, when all the vegetables are tender–crisp, pour it into the skillet and gently stir in the meat or tofu. Continue cooking until the vegetables are glazed and the sauce slightly thickens. Do not overcook a cornstarch-thickened sauce; it reverts to being thin again. (If you are stir-frying a large amount of food, you may want to use more marinade to sauce it.)

FOR BAKING OR BARBECUING

Be sure to marinate the chicken, fish or tofu for at least 30 minutes. Drain and reserve marinade; use for basting.

Dipping Sauce for Brassicas—

- ☐ 2 tablespoons plain low-fat yogurt
- ☐ 2 tablespoons low-fat cottage cheese
- ☐ 2 tablespoons mayonnaise
- ☐ ½ teaspoon Dijon-type mustard, or to taste
- ☐ ¼ teaspoon soy sauce, or to taste

—is a low-fat sauce in which to dunk cool or warm cauliflower, broccoli and Brussels sprouts.

Whirl the ingredients together in a blender if you want a smooth sauce. Otherwise, just stir the ingredients together thoroughly and serve. Enough for 2 servings.

Salsa—

- ☐ 2 large, ripe tomatoes
- ☐ 1 clove garlic, pressed
- ☐ 2 teaspoons minced fresh cilantro
- ☐ 1 small red onion
- ☐ 1 jalapeño pepper or 2 serrano chilies
- ☐ juice of ½ lime
- ☐ salt and pepper to taste

—to top your tostadas, huevos rancheros, refried beans, or to use as a dip for tortilla chips.

Finely chop the chilies or pepper, tomatoes, cilantro and onion. Stir well with remaining ingredients. Adjust seasonings to taste. Will keep for a week in the refrigerator. Can be made in larger quantity and frozen in appropriate-sized containers.

Chunky Herbed Tomato Sauce—

- ☐ 1 small yellow onion, chopped
- ☐ 1 clove garlic, minced
- ☐ 1 ½ tablespoons minced fresh basil or 1 teaspoon dried basil
- ☐ ½ teaspoon dried oregano
- ☐ 4 tablespoons vermouth or dry white wine
- ☐ 1 ½ lbs. fresh or 1 28-oz. can whole peeled tomatoes, chopped
- ☐ 1 6-oz. can tomato paste
- ☐ Salt and pepper to taste

—to top pasta or wherever a marinara sauce is needed.

In a saucepan with a tight-fitting lid, sauté the onion, garlic, and herbs in the wine. When the onion is soft, stir in the tomatoes and tomato paste. Bring to a boil. Reduce heat; simmer uncovered 5 to 10 minutes. Salt and pepper to taste.

This recipe can easily be doubled and the extra portion of sauce frozen in 8-oz. yogurt containers; 1 cup tomato sauce will top 8 ounces, or 2 servings, of pasta.

The Quickest Herbed Tomato Sauce—

- ☐ 1 medium onion, chopped
- ☐ 1 clove garlic, minced
- ☐ 2 tablespoons olive oil
- ☐ 1 15-oz. can of tomato sauce
- ☐ ¼ teaspoon dried basil
- ☐ ¼ teaspoon freshly ground pepper

—can be served with stuffed cannelloni, lasagna, tempeh, veal or chicken dishes—wherever a marinara sauce is called for. Despite its simplicity, this is a rich-tasting, flavorful tomato sauce.

In a covered saucepan, sauté the onion and garlic in the olive oil until the onion is soft. Stir occasionally, making sure the onion or garlic doesn't brown. Stir in the remaining ingredients. Bring to just below boiling point and serve.

This recipe can be easily doubled and the extra sauce frozen in 8-oz. yogurt containers; 1 cup sauce will top 8 ounces, or 2 servings, of pasta.

APPENDIX IV

Breakfast

We all know breakfast is important, perhaps more important than any other meal of the day. Yet finding fresh ideas for the daily, time-constricted breakfast is difficult.

Following are some ideas for preparing nutritious breakfasts. There are suggestions on how to more easily prepare whole grain hot cereal. The unusual egg recipes describe ways of including eggs in your diet without raising your cholesterol intake above its limits. And, although some of the recipes for muffins, breakfast cobblers and puddings take as long as an hour to prepare, a one-time cooking effort in the evening or on the weekend will provide you with pleasant breakfasts for the work week.

But first—a word about fiber.

Fiber

Breakfast seems to be when most people think about including fiber in their diet, so they ritualistically sprinkle a bit of bran on this or that as if it were a talisman against "modern ills." Wait a minute. What *is* dietary fiber? What does it do? Is bran the only source?

Dietary fiber is, by definition, any plant material we ingest that the human gut cannot break down. There are actually two types of dietary fiber—cellulosic and soluble fiber; each performs a different function in the body. Cellulosic fiber absorbs water and provides bulk to keep things moving through the gastro-intestinal tract. Bran, which is actually a generic term referring to the outer coating of any grain, provides cellulosic fiber. In whole grain products such as brown rice, whole wheat flour, and whole barley, the bran remains. Refined products (white rice, pearl barley, white flour) have been stripped of their bran.

The other type of fiber includes mucilage, gums and pectin. These soluble fibers serve to stabilize blood sugar levels, lower the level of fat and cholesterol in the blood, and may improve the absorption of water soluble vitamins (Vitamin C and the B vitamins). Apples, blackberries, pears, strawberries and plums have the highest percentage of soluble fiber of all the fruits; in vegetables, the highest percentages are in peas, broccoli, zucchini, summer squash, carrots and tomatoes. Oatmeal is very high in mucilage (that's why it's so gummy), as are rye, barley, okra, sesame seeds and *all* the legumes.

The usefulness of pectic substances is affected by the way food is prepared. Juicing fruits and vegetables leaves almost no pectic fiber; puréeing greatly reduces the amount of fiber, as does boiling. It is better to steam vegetables and to leave fruits and vegetables unpeeled.

A high fiber diet is extremely helpful in weight control because high fiber foods are low in calories yet their bulk makes you feel full. Refined foods, on the other hand, are often highly caloric but not filling. High fiber foods take up space in your stomach, absorb a great deal of water, and slow down digestion, so you feel satiated longer and consume fewer calories than if you'd eaten refined foods.

Eating a diet of whole foods, not just sprinkling bran in your granola, will provide you with a high fiber diet. Because of fiber's many benefits, perhaps it is a modern talisman after all.

CEREALS

Hot Cereal

SERVES 3 TO 4

☐ *1 cup rolled oats or coarser grains (i.e. cracked wheat, flaked rye)*
☐ *3 cups nonfat milk or water*
☐ *¼ teaspoon salt*

If you don't have whole grain hot cereals for breakfasts because you can't find the time, patience and/or organization to cook them, here are two cooking techniques which may be helpful.

I. THE THERMOS METHOD

Before you go to sleep, bring the milk or water to a boil and put into a wide-mouthed thermos along with the cereal and salt. Add cut-up dried fruit or raisins, if you'd like. The cereal will be cooked and warm the next morning. If it is too thick, stir in some milk until it is the right consistency. Sweeten to taste. This is a useful method when you are camping or boating.

II. THE CROCKPOT METHOD

Rub the inside of the Crockpot with a pat of butter. Bring the water or milk to a boil on the stove. Stir the milk or water, cereal, salt, and optional dried fruit or raisins into the Crockpot. Cover and cook on the low setting overnight. This method makes it easy to cook hot cereal for a number of people and keep it warm and on hand for different morning schedules.

Granola

Store-bought granola is often stale and oversweetened, the oil tastes rancid and if it has raisins, they've been toasted along with the oatmeal to make for hard little pellets between your teeth. In about 8 minutes, you can assemble the ingredients to make a large store of delicious homemade granola. Not only will your cereal taste infinitely better than anything you can buy, it will cost you much less. The only trick is that it must be stirred every 10 minutes as it toasts. You must be very faithful to this chore; charring a whole batch of granola is a terrible experience. Set a timer if need be.

Here is a basic recipe which can be varied with the addition of different nuts, seeds, and dried fruits.

☐ *1 cup sunflower seeds, shelled*
☐ *1 cup sesame seeds, unhulled*
☐ *¼ cup honey or brown sugar*
☐ *¼ cup light vegetable oil*
☐ *1 teaspoon vanilla extract*
☐ *½ cup bran*
☐ *4 cups rolled oats*
☐ *2 cups toasted wheat germ*

Put the sunflower seeds in a large shallow baking pan in the middle shelf of a 300° oven. Shake the pan every 5 minutes until the seeds are slightly golden. Remove to a bowl. Repeat this process with the sesame seeds.

While the seeds are toasting, warm the honey in a saucepan until it is thin; stir in the oil. If you are using brown sugar, just stir together the sugar and oil. Add the vanilla extract. In a large bowl, mix together the bran and oats. Pour the oil mixture over the oats and bran and distribute it evenly with either your hands or a large spoon.

Spread this mixture in the baking pan and place it on the middle shelf of the 300° oven. Stir every 10 minutes for 45 minutes, or until the oats are golden. Remove from oven and stir in the seeds and toasted wheat germ. Cool. Store in tightly covered containers in the refrigerator.

EGG DISHES

The American Heart Association has set the maximum safe intake of cholesterol at 300 mg. per day. A single egg yolk provides 250 to 300 mg. of cholesterol—your whole day's allotment. There is, of course, cholesterol in other foods you'd normally eat in a day—meat, butter, and dairy products, for example. That is why it is generally advised to reduce the number of eggs one eats to three or four per week.

This all seems fairly straightforward, until you look at the egg studies. When healthy young men are fed lots of eggs—the equivalent of up to 900 mg. of cholesterol per day, most of them (over 80%) show little or no increase in the level of cholesterol in their blood. Apparently there are responders and nonresponders to the cholesterol in egg yolks, and most of us are nonresponders.

You could, with a doctor's help, find out if you are a "responder" by monitoring your cholesterol count as you experiment with your diet. But few of us are going to do that. Instead, you are left in a kind of Russian Roulette situation—you simply don't know if the cholesterol in eggs will raise your blood cholesterol levels or not.

To be safe, the following recipes "extend" eggs so that fewer are eaten. Incorporating tofu with eggs is an excellent way of extending eggs. Tofu complements the texture of egg but is neutral in taste. It takes on whatever flavors and seasonings you add. Sprinkle in basil, marjoram and thyme for a savory dish; soy sauce, grated ginger and green onions for an Oriental flavor; or, lots of sautéed onions and some grated cheese for a rich, hearty breakfast.

Another way to enjoy eggs without raising your cholesterol intake beyond its limits is to omit some or all of the yolks. Egg whites are high in protein but cholesterol-free. A substitution of two egg whites for one whole egg works for most recipes. For a "Three Egg Omelette," you could use 6 egg whites, or 4 egg whites plus 1 whole egg. Give the extra yolks to your cat or dog instead of canned food. You won't feel as if you are wasting food and their coats will soon be luxuriant and shiny.

Spicy Tofu Hash and Eggs

SERVES 4

TIME TO PREPARE

10 minutes

- ☐ 2 tablespoons oil
- ☐ 16 oz. tofu
- ☐ ½ teaspoon dill weed
- ☐ ½ teaspoon garlic powder
- ☐ ¼ teaspoon each turmeric, salt, thyme, basil, ground cumin, curry powder
- ☐ 1 ½ tablespoons soy sauce
- ☐ 4 whole eggs

Slice the tofu horizontally into thin slabs and press between layers of paper towel. Heat the oil in a large skillet. Sauté the tofu over medium high heat, breaking it up with a spatula. Sprinkle with soy sauce and herbs and stir for a minute. Reduce heat to medium low. Move the tofu to the side of the skillet to make room for the eggs. Add a film of oil or butter to the skillet; fry the eggs "over easy." Divide the tofu amongst 4 warm plates and top each serving with a fried egg.

Tofu prepared this way is also delicious stuffed into pita bread.

Jay's Fried Tortillas and Eggs

SERVES 1

(easily increased)

TIME TO PREPARE

10 minutes

- ☐ 2 corn tortillas, cut or torn into 1 × 1-inch pieces
- ☐ 1 egg, lightly beaten
- ☐ ¼ cup diced cheese (Farmer's, Jack or mild cheddar)
- ☐ vegetable oil
- ☐ salsa or taco sauce

In larger quantities, this makes a fast brunch or lunch for unexpected guests, or a pleasant light supper. Although mild cheddar or Jack cheese could be used in this recipe, I recommend Farmer's cheese. It is a low-fat cheese that tastes just like Jack in cooked dishes.

Over medium high heat in a skillet very lightly coated with oil, stir-fry the tortilla pieces until they are golden. Lightly salt the tortillas. Stir in the egg and cheese. Stir until the egg is set and the cheese melted. Serve on a warm plate with salsa or taco sauce.

This recipe can be enhanced with diced bell peppers, zucchini, onions, jalapeño peppers, tomatoes, and a garnish of chopped cilantro. Lightly sauté the vegetables in a little oil until slightly softened. Add to the lightly beaten eggs. Wipe out the skillet and fry the tortillas until golden. Pour in the eggs, cheese and sautéed vegetables and cook until the eggs are set.

Fast and Simple Tofu and Eggs

SERVES 2

TIME TO PREPARE

10 minutes

- ☐ *8 oz. firm tofu*
- ☐ *2 whole eggs, or 4 egg whites, lightly beaten*
- ☐ *soy sauce to taste*
- ☐ *1 tablespoon vegetable oil*
- ☐ *finely minced cilantro and green onions or chives*

Slice the tofu horizontally into thin slabs and press dry between paper towels. Heat oil over medium high heat; begin to fry the tofu. Chop the cilantro and onions and beat the eggs. With a spatula, break up the tofu into small pieces and sprinkle generously with soy sauce. Pour the eggs over the tofu and toss until the eggs are set. Serve on warm plates; garnish with chopped greenery. A sprinkle of toasted sesame seeds is good, too.

Scrambled Zucchini Frittata

SERVES 1

TIME TO PREPARE

10 minutes

- ☐ *1 teaspoon olive oil*
- ☐ *1 small zucchini, grated*
- ☐ *1 whole egg, or 2 egg whites, lightly beaten*
- ☐ *a pinch each of dried basil and oregano*
- ☐ *2 tablespoons grated cheese (Farmer's, Jack, or mild cheddar)*
- ☐ *freshly ground pepper to taste*

Heat the olive oil in a small skillet. Stir-fry the grated zucchini for a minute. Lightly beat the eggs with the herbs. Pour in the eggs and stir until they are set. Stir in the grated cheese at the very end. Season with freshly ground pepper.

WHOLE GRAIN MUFFINS

Home-baked muffins make a simple breakfast seem a treat. They also have the advantage of being portable; in a pinch, one can breakfast on muffins and a thermos of milk on the bus or at the office. Perhaps the greatest advantage, though, is that muffins provide an alternative for people who'd *never* eat cereal for breakfast. People who hate oatmeal porridge love oatmeal muffins!

Although they initially take time to prepare, it's well worth it. A one-time baking effort can provide for several days. Or, a supply of muffins can be stored in the freezer. Muffins should be frozen while they are still warm from baking. Reheat them at 350° for 15 or 20 minutes in a brown paper bag that you've sprinkled with water.

BAKING TIPS
♦ Use paper liners or teflon-coated muffin tins. They speed up preparation and clean-up time.
♦ Leave the top third of muffin cups unfilled. Baked goods that rely on baking soda as the leavening agent need a wall to climb.
♦ Don't try to save energy by putting muffins into an oven that isn't preheated. They won't rise properly.
♦ Put a little water in the empty muffin cups; the muffins remain moist as they bake.
♦ Recipes can be varied by using different flours or spices, by adding seeds or nuts, minced dried or fresh fruit, or leftover cooked grains, or by substituting fruit juice, buttermilk or yogurt for the liquid. The following muffin recipes demonstrate a range of possibilities. Try these, then experiment, keeping the recipes' proportions in mind.

Perfect Bran Muffins

MAKES 12 TO 18 MUFFINS

TIME TO PREPARE

40 minutes

☐ *2 tablespoons butter*
☐ *2 tablespoons vegetable oil*
☐ *¼ cup (4 tablespoons) honey*
☐ *¼ cup (4 tablespoons) molasses*
☐ *1 cup nonfat or whole milk*
☐ *2 eggs, lightly beaten*
☐ *1 ½ cups bran*
☐ *1 cup whole wheat flour*
☐ *1 ½ teaspoons baking soda*
☐ *½ teaspoon salt*
☐ *½ cup raisins*

If you are trying to lower the proportion of calories in your daily diet provided by fat, you may be interested in these figures. A cup of nonfat milk has 71 calories and .2 grams fat; 1 cup of whole milk has 159 calories and 8.5 grams fat. You can use either in this recipe.

Preheat the oven to 400°. Oil the muffin cups or prepare with paper liners. Over medium heat, warm the butter, oil, honey and molasses. When this mixture is blended and thin, remove from heat. Stir in the milk and then the eggs. Add the bran.

In a large bowl, sift together the flour, baking soda and salt. Stir in the raisins, coating them with flour so that they are separated. Form a well in the center of these ingredients and pour in the liquid mixture. Mix together thoroughly but gently. Fill the muffin cups ⅔ full. Bake 25 minutes, or until done. Cool on a rack.

Multi-Grain Muffins

MAKES 1 DOZEN

TIME TO PREPARE

40 minutes

- ☐ ⅓ *cup soy flour*
- ☐ ⅓ *cup cornmeal*
- ☐ *1 cup whole wheat flour*
- ☐ ¼ *cup sesame seeds*
- ☐ ½ *teaspoon salt*
- ☐ *1 tablespoon grated orange rind*
- ☐ *1 ½ teaspoon baking soda*
- ☐ ⅔ *cup plain low-fat yogurt or buttermilk*
- ☐ *1 egg, lightly beaten*
- ☐ *4 tablespoons melted butter or 2 tablespoons melted butter plus 2 tablespoons light vegetable oil*
- ☐ ⅓ *cup honey*

Preheat the oven to 350°. Lightly oil the muffin cups or prepare with paper liners. Stir together the soy flour, cornmeal, wheat flour, sesame seeds, salt, orange rind and baking soda. In a separate bowl, mix together the yogurt or buttermilk and egg. Melt the butter in a saucepan; add the honey and oil, if you are using any. Stir this into the yogurt and egg mixture.

Form a well in the dry ingredients. Pour the liquid ingredients into it. Stir together gently but thoroughly. Fill the muffin cups ⅔ full and bake 25 minutes, or until done.

Oatmeal Muffins

MAKES 1 ½ DOZEN

TIME TO PREPARE

55 minutes

- ☐ *1 ¼ cups whole wheat flour*
- ☐ *1 ½ cups rolled oats, chopped in a blender or food processor*
- ☐ *2 tablespoons wheat germ or bran*
- ☐ ½ *cup sunflower seeds*
- ☐ *1 teaspoon cinnamon*
- ☐ *1 ¼ teaspoon baking soda*
- ☐ ½ *cup raisins*
- ☐ *2 medium-sized apples, unpeeled, coarsely grated*
- ☐ *2 tablespoons butter*
- ☐ ⅓ *cup honey*
- ☐ *2 cups buttermilk or 2 tablespoons fresh lemon juice plus nonfat milk to equal 2 cups*
- ☐ *1 egg, lightly beaten*

Oatmeal is an outstanding source of mucilaginous fiber which recent studies show stabilizes blood sugar levels and lowers the level of cholesterol in the blood. If you aren't particularly fond of oatmeal porridge, these dense, moist muffins are a delicious way to incorporate oatmeal into your diet.

Preheat oven to 375°. Lightly oil 18 muffin cups or prepare with paper liners. In a large bowl, combine flour, oats, wheat germ or bran, sunflower seeds, cinnamon and baking soda. Mix in the raisins and grated apple so that they are coated with flour and evenly distributed.

In a saucepan, melt the butter. Remove from heat and stir in the oil and honey. Mix together the buttermilk and egg; add to the honey and butter. Mix thoroughly. Make a well in the dry ingredients and pour in the liquid ingredients. Combine gently but thoroughly. Fill the muffin cups ¾ full. These muffins rise very little. Bake for 35 minutes, or until done. Remove from the oven. Transfer the muffins to a rack to cool.

Some desserts are really meals in themselves that one could eat in good conscience for breakfast: rice pudding, bread pudding, fruit cobblers with whole grain toppings, and baked apples, for example. The amount of honey or sugar in the following recipes has been reduced so that they are not dessert sweet.

Compote

There is something soothing about compote on a gray winter's day, all of a summer's sunshine stored within the glistening fruit. A small serving can top hot cereal. Or couple compote with ricotta cheese and spread on toast or muffins. You could use any dried fruits or combination of fruits to make a compote. My favorite is apricots. A bit of grated or slivered lemon peel and blanched almonds could also be added. Here are two different methods for making compote:

☐ ½ lb. dried fruits (apricots, peaches, dates, apples, raisins, etc.)
☐ ½ tablespoon grated orange peel

I. Put the ingredients into a saucepan and barely cover with water. Bring to a boil. Cover and simmer until the fruit is soft and plump, or about 10 minutes. (Some dried fruits will take twice that long to plump.) Cool, and refrigerate.

II. Put the fruit into a canning jar. Pour enough boiling water over the fruit so that it is covered and there is 1 inch of water above the fruit. Cover with a clean towel or cheese cloth and let sit for 36 to 48 hours. When the fruit is swollen and soft, refrigerate.

Fresh Fruit and Cheese

SERVES 2

TIME TO PREPARE

5 minutes

☐ *3 heaping tablespoons low-fat cottage cheese or ricotta*
☐ *3 heaping tablespoons plain low-fat yogurt*
☐ *2 teaspoons honey*
☐ *juice of ½ orange*
☐ *½ orange, peeled, seeded and sectioned*
☐ *1 small apple, diced*
☐ *1 small banana, diced*
☐ *1 small pear, diced*
☐ *toasted wheat germ*
☐ *chopped nuts*

Combine the cheese, yogurt, honey and orange juice. Prepare the fruit and divide between two bowls. Top with yogurt mixture. Sprinkle with wheat germ and chopped nuts.

Uncooked Applesauce

MAKES 1 ½ CUPS

TIME TO PREPARE

5 minutes

☐ *3 apples*
☐ *¼ cup apple juice or orange juice*

Core and coarsely dice apples. Put apples and juice into a food processor or blender and purée thoroughly.

Cooked Applesauce

MAKES 1 QUART

TIME TO PREPARE

15 minutes, 45 minutes to cook (or cook overnight in Crockpot)

☐ *10 large apples, cored and thinly sliced*
☐ *¼ teaspoon cinnamon*
☐ *¼ cup apple juice or 2 tablespoons water plus 2 tablespoons honey*
☐ *3 tablespoons lemon juice*

Using an electric slow cooker is the easiest way to cook applesauce because you don't have to worry about scorching the bottom of the pot. To cook apples on the stove top, set a heat absorbing waffle under the pot; this will prevent scorching and you won't have to stir the pot as often.

Put all the ingredients except the lemon juice into the pot. Cover. If you are using a Crockpot, turn it to the slow setting and leave overnight or longer, until the apples are cooked. If you are cooking on top of the stove, cook over medium high heat if you have a heat absorbing waffle, or medium low heat if you don't. Stir every 15 minutes—more often if you've no heat waffle. Check for doneness after 45 minutes.

After the apples are cooked and have cooled slightly, stir in the lemon juice and taste. Do you want to add more honey? More lemon juice? Does it need more liquid?

Applesauce will keep for 2 weeks in the refrigerator.

Breakfast Cobbler

SERVES 6

TIME TO PREPARE

55 minutes

- ☐ *6 cups apples, thinly sliced*
- ☐ *½ teaspoon cinnamon*
- ☐ *½ cup honey*
- ☐ *juice of ½ lemon*

- ☐ *3 cups apples, coarsely diced*
- ☐ *¾ cup honey*
- ☐ *12 oz. cranberries*
- ☐ *¼ cup grated orange rind*
- ☐ *2 teaspoons almond extract*

- ☐ *¾ cup rolled oats*
- ☐ *½ cup cornmeal*
- ☐ *2 tablespoons honey*
- ☐ *1 teaspoon cinnamon*
- ☐ *3 tablespoons butter*
- ☐ *¼ to ½ cup coarsely chopped walnuts or almonds*

- ☐ *1 teaspoon cinnamon*
- ☐ *1 cup wheat germ*
- ☐ *3 tablespoons butter*
- ☐ *¼ to ½ cup coarsely chopped walnuts or almonds*

Top each serving of cobbler with plain low-fat yogurt.

FILLING I

Combine the ingredients thoroughly. Spoon into a large, buttered casserole. Sprinkle with TOPPING I or II. Cover with foil and bake at 425° for 40 minutes, or until the apples are soft. Remove the foil for the last 10 minutes of baking.

FILLING II

Mix together the ingredients. Spread into a buttered 2 quart baking dish. Sprinkle with TOPPING I or II. Cover with foil and bake at 425° for 40 minutes. Remove the foil for the last 10 minutes of baking.

TOPPING I

In a medium-sized saucepan, warm the butter and honey. When they are blended and runny, remove from heat. Stir in the cornmeal and oats. Mix thoroughly. Sprinkle over the filling. Bake as directed.

TOPPING II

Combine the cinnamon and wheat germ. Sprinkle over the filling. Dot with butter. Bake as directed.

Stuffed Baked Apples

SERVES 5

TIME TO PREPARE

1 hour to bake (or cook 6 hours in Crockpot)

- ☐ *5 large green apples*
- ☐ *1 ½ tablespoons honey*
- ☐ *1 ½ tablespoons tahini or nut butter*
- ☐ *1 tablespoon white wine or sake*
- ☐ *1 tablespoon miso (see page 105)*
- ☐ *1 tablespoon soft butter*
- ☐ *¼ teaspoon cinnamon*
- ☐ *¼ cup raisins*

Preheat the oven to 350°. Core the apples, but leave the bottom intact so that the filling won't flow out. Stir together the remaining ingredients and stuff into the apples. Wrap in foil and bake on cookie sheet 35 to 40 minutes, or until the apples yield to a squeeze. If you are using an electric slow cooker, stack wrapped apples in pot; cover and cook on low setting 6 hours, or overnight.

Bread Pudding

SERVES 8

TIME TO PREPARE

50 minutes

- ☐ *4 cups coarsely crumbled stale bread (collect heels and stale pieces of bread in a heavy plastic bag in the freezer)*
- ☐ *3 to 4 apples (1 ½ cups grated)*
- ☐ *½ cup raisins or other cut-up dried fruit*
- ☐ *½ cup chopped nuts*
- ☐ *3 cups nonfat milk*
- ☐ *3 eggs*
- ☐ *2 teaspoons vanilla extract*
- ☐ *6 tablespoons honey*
- ☐ *½ teaspoon cinnamon*
- ☐ *½ teaspoon salt*
- ☐ *¼ teaspoon nutmeg*
- ☐ *juice of ½ lemon*

Preheat the oven to 350°. In a baking pan, mix the bread crumbs, grated apple, dried fruit and nuts. Combine the rest of the ingredients in a blender or processor and pour over the dry mixture. Make sure the bread is saturated. Bake for 35 minutes.

Bread pudding will keep for 5 days in the refrigerator. It is good topped with applesauce or compote and plain yogurt.

Nearly Instant Rice Pudding

SERVES 1

TIME TO PREPARE

10 minutes

☐ *½ cup cooked rice*
☐ *½ cup nonfat milk*
☐ *1 tablespoon toasted wheat germ*
☐ *2 tablespoons raisins*
☐ *2 tablespoons broken walnuts, almonds, or sunflower seeds*
☐ *1 teaspoon molasses*

Combine all the ingredients in a saucepan and cook over low heat. Simmer covered for 5 minutes.

Pumpkin Pudding

SERVES 6

TIME TO PREPARE

40 to 45 minutes

☐ *16 oz. low-fat cottage cheese*
☐ *⅛ teaspoon salt*
☐ *2 cups canned pumpkin*
☐ *4 eggs*
☐ *4 tablespoons honey*
☐ *¼ teaspoon nutmeg*

Preheat the oven to 350°. Put all the ingredients except the nutmeg in a blender or processor. Blend until smooth. Pour into individual custard cups or one baking dish. Place the baking dish or cups into a pan of warm water and bake 35 to 40 minutes, or until firm. Sprinkle with nutmeg and chill before serving.

INDEX